HERE I AM: A JEW IN TODAY'S GERMANY

HERE I AM:
A JEW
IN TODAY'S
GERMANY

by IRVING HALPERIN

W
THE WESTMINSTER PRESS
Philadelphia

ISBN 0-664-20899-1

LIBRARY OF CONGRESS CATALOG CARD NO. 76-134872

PUBLISHED BY THE WESTMINSTER PRESS ®
PHILADELPHIA, PENNSYLVANIA

PRINTED IN THE UNITED STATES OF AMERICA

To my children,
DANIEL, DINA, JONATHAN,
in a more humane world

ACKNOWLEDGMENTS

Brief parts of this book, in different form, have appeared in *The Christian Century, Congress Bi-Weekly, Jewish Frontier,* and *World Jewry.*

For permission to quote material, I must thank *Commentary* (quotations from Professor Gershom Scholem's "Jews and Germans"). Copyright © 1966 by the American Jewish Committee.

I feel especially grateful to my wife, who has worked with me, listening, reading, clarifying, and, as always, providing sustenance.

I. H.

CONTENTS

I

INSIDE GERMANY: FIRST DAYS

THOSE FIRST HOURS inside Germany. . . . Night shrouded
the land. Paris was hours behind us. The train moved beside villages, small towns. I saw very few lights. A place of sullen darkness. They are sleeping, I thought, and can't see us. How
strange that we were entering their land with impunity! Here,
twenty years earlier, my family and I would have been boxed up
within a transport car. Now, like guerrillas invading enemy territory under the cover of night, we were advancing into Germany. Through the windows of our coach, the passing shapes of
houses looked grim, hard-bitten.

I felt no urge to cry out, "Wake up—Jews are entering!"
When a middle-aged conductor came to punch my ticket, I did
not explode the words *"Ich bin ein Jude"* into his face. Even the
cliché question—where was he during those years?—did not
occur to me then. The sound of his voice, of German, grated.
He grunted something, punched my ticket, and passed on.

Since space enough for all of us to sit together had not been
available, my wife, daughter, and youngest son were in an adjoining car. I guessed that Dina and Jon were asleep. Perhaps
Tam was also looking out of a window, thinking about how it
would be for us in the months ahead. Or she may have been recalling her deceased father's hatred of Germans, the bitterness
with which he had often spoken about them. No, he would not
have countenanced fine distinctions: young Germans, old Ger-

mans, guilty ones, innocent ones. . . . They, Germans, en masse, were not to be trusted ever again. He wished only that "they should go to hell." And now his daughter and her family were going to *that* accursed place! Were he alive, perhaps he would have come at me with burning eyes, asking, "Why are you taking my daughter *there*—to a place of murderers?"

My family and I got to Germany because I had applied for a Fulbright grant to Israel. In January of 1963 I received a form letter from Washington, D.C., indicating that I had been nominated for a Fulbright lecturer's grant to Israel. True, the writer of the letter did specify that a nomination does not necessarily result in an appointment. The Fulbright Commission in Israel, an English Department at one of the universities there, and a committee in Washington would have to pass favorably on my candidacy. Still, when I checked with a colleague who had had a Fulbright to another country, he said: "You're as good as in. A nomination is a 95 percent guarantee of an appointment." So I exulted. Israel again after an absence of nine years!

Tam and I dreamed, prepared. She had as much reason as I for looking forward. Years before, as a young Zionist, she had seriously thought of emigrating to Israel. But later, as her direction led to universities in Chicago and then to a career in social work, the dream of Israel gradually receded. In 1955, shortly after we met in Chicago, I said that I would take her to Israel someday. The year before, I had briefly visited the country for the first time and had been bitten by whatever it is that bites you there, so that you have to keep returning.

But the nomination for a Fulbright grant to Israel did not turn into an appointment. I got a regret-to-say letter from a Washington official. It seemed that my academic speciality did not coincide with the needs of the Fulbright program in Israel.

I agonized, but to no avail.

What next? Apparently someone in the Fulbright operation circulated my papers, because I got a phone call from Washington. Was I interested in the possibility of a post in Teheran?

Teheran! I was not. So then perhaps someone noticed that my
application indicated an emergent interest in the literature of
the European Holocaust and concluded that Germany would be
fitting territory for me. Anyway, whatever the explanation, the
fact is that in the early summer of 1963, the Fulbright Commission in Bad Godesberg notified me that I had been nominated
for a lectureship to Germany.

I felt certain that this time the nomination would not
backfire. To Germany we would go *if* this was what we wanted.
Why the qualification? Because, for one, my wife was less than
enthusiastic about the prospect. "Why do you want to go *there*
after what happened to European Jewry?" she asked. A part of
my conscious motive stemmed from a program we both had recently seen on TV—a group of young Germans on the way to
visit Dachau. The commentator referred to their visit as a pilgrimage of penance. The faces of these young people were
grave. Walking along a road, they sang a Hebrew song. I wondered about them. Still, at that remove in geography, I could
hardly be certain that their public atonement was truly genuine
and not cheaply sentimental. Perhaps it was too easy for them
to feel a sense of "collective shame."

There was, however, a not so noble reason for wanting to go
to Germany. A Fulbright grant would make it possible for Tam
and me to travel, to see Europe. After several consecutive years
of teaching, I badly needed a change of pace, of setting. Also, it
titillated my imagination to speculate on the possibilities of danger and high adventure in former (and maybe still?) enemy territory. But beyond these inclinations, both banal and theatrical,
given my developing interest in the history and the literature of
the Holocaust, I wanted to have a concrete, close-up sense of
Germany and Germans. I was especially curious to hear what
young Germans thought about Hitler, National Socialism, Israel, the question of so-called collective guilt, and the problems
of German-Jewish reconciliation. Additionally, the thought
vaguely occurred to me that I might be able to do some good
(though what this "good" might conceivably be eluded my con-

scious understanding at the time) in Germany as a publicly identified Jew.

One day in July an envelope displaying a German postage stamp arrived. I placed the envelope on a table while Tam, looking tense, stood beside me. The letter indicated that I was being offered an appointment as a lecturer of American literature in the English Seminar at the University of Erlangen-Nuremberg.

I was not displeased. Tam, however, was less than ecstatic. A year in France or Italy or Denmark she could look forward to. But Germany! Yes, and with three young children—one of them still in diapers—to look after. . . .

When I informed my mother, her first response was: "How can you risk the lives of your family? You'll go to a doctor there with one of the children," she continued, greatly agitated. "Somehow he'll realize you're a Jew. Under the Nazis, maybe he killed our people in medical experiments. Would you entrust your children to such a doctor? Think what you're doing! Think!"

I replied that such a possibility would never have occurred to me, that one needed to have trust, good faith. She shook her head. Years back she had fled Russia because of the pogroms, and here was her son choosing to go to the country that had had the biggest pogrom of them all.

When Tam and I first told our friends the news, it was as though they hadn't heard us. Because I had been involved in lecturing and writing on the Holocaust, their shock on hearing of our decision was understandable. In their view, Tam and I ought to have boycotted Germany, as they did Franco Spain.

I can't say now that I anticipated having no future misgivings over my acceptance of this Fulbright assignment. Once on German soil, we might well find that our reactions to certain Germans would be highly "unobjective," if not irrational. Still, I didn't believe—perhaps didn't want to—that this possibility constituted reason enough for rejecting the invitation.

In any case, I simply couldn't be satisfied with the naturalistic

explanation that the relationship between the German assignment and my original application to Israel was merely coinci-
dental, a manifestation of the contingent. Rather, I was at-
tracted to the mystique of the saying: "Man proposes, but God
disposes." In short, I sensed that it was right and ripe for us to
go there and learn what there was to learn.

Wheels moved under us. Our oldest boy lay asleep in my lap.
Travel-weary, he was not to awake until we reached Nuremberg
early the next morning. From the spectral shapes of passing
houses, I heard an occasional dim voice, sometimes sinister
sounds.

Suddenly I was angry with myself for having exposed my
family to the uncertainties ahead. The warnings of my mother
came back. The guarded faces of our friends, when we told
them the news, came back. I had attempted to explain, to justify
our decision with such exalted language as Pilgrimage, Mission,
To Do a Job as a Committed Jew. . . . But sitting in the dark-
ened train, I admitted to myself that I felt no such lofty commitment.

Danny stirred, he felt feverish, and his lips moved, as though
he were thirsty. The coach compartment was hot, rank. But if I
rose now to open a window, he might awake, and, given our
midnight departure from Paris, my son badly needed sleep. Nor
was it simply a matter of going to the window and opening it.
Others, strangers, sat beside and across from us. Earlier, before
Danny fell asleep on my lap, I had opened the window slightly.
Whereupon it had been promptly closed by an elderly gentleman sitting beside me. Vexed, he muttered something in German. When he rose and went to the window, I noticed that he
had one leg.

Throughout the trip I never saw his face clearly. Only one
quality of it is lodged in my memory—an embittered expression. Did he lose the leg in the war? Whatever the explanation, I did not feel pity for the man sitting beside us in the
overheated compartment. He sat like a log, with his leg jammed

hard against my thigh, as though in a deliberate act of spite. Beside him sat an elderly woman, possibly his wife. There wasn't room for any of us to stretch out on the seat. Change seats? Every one in the car was occupied.

I continued to feel concern for Danny, and for his younger sister and brother in the next compartment. All the pulling this way and that in ships, planes, and trains over the weeks since our departure from San Francisco. Nosebleeds, coughs, colds, lumpy hotel beds, had been their lot. And why? Because their parents had willfully chosen to rearrange drastically the settings and conditions of their lives. What also may have been troubling to them—at least to Danny—is that we were going to live in the same country where the bad man Hitler, the murderer of Jews, had lived. So that perhaps someday Danny and his sister and brother would ask of Tam and me, "Why did you take us there?" What then would we answer?

I thought again about the Germans whom we would be meeting. Certainly my best friend's advice—not to preach at them, not to accuse, not to interrogate—was sensible. "Listen," he said, "just listen." He and I sharply disagreed with the point of view expressed by a mutual acquaintance, a man known for his aggressiveness, who had said to me: "Don't go there on your knees. From the outset, tell them who you are, a Jew. If I were going there, I would challenge them to knock my head off if they dared."

My friend's advice was convincing, but would I be able to settle for being only the listener, the observer?

Well, in the beginning, aboard the *Queen Mary,* which took us to Europe, I had played it fairly cool in the company of a young German who worked for the American Embassy in Bonn. He was accompanying us, the Fulbright grantees, to Cherbourg. He seemed intelligent, likable, and I especially recall a brief conversation we had on the last morning of the voyage. I brought up the subject of anti-Semitism in postwar Germany. He was convinced that it was no longer a problem there. "The German people are truly sorry," he said, "and wish to make amends." His reply wasn't to my satisfaction.

And what of swastika episodes in Cologne? I thought. And the noisy reunions of former members of the SS? And the polls in Germany indicating that the majority of the people wanted to "forget" the war crimes of the recent past? I might have pressed these questions but chose not to. At the time it seemed to me that a guest-to-be in his country—yes, and a Jew (having ready access to my Fulbright dossier with its description of my interest in Israel, Jewish publications, etc., he could adduce as much) to boot—ought not, on so brief an acquaintanceship, to press such "sensitive" questions.

A day later, aboard a ship train from Cherbourg to Paris, our youngest son, Jonathan, then three, played with a middle-aged, obese, affluent-looking German who sat across from our family in the compartment. "I would like to hold your boy," he said. What should I have said to him? No, don't touch my son, because I don't know what you did during the Hitler years. Should I have said point-blank, "We are *Juden,* and your people murdered 1,500,000 Jewish children"? At the time I felt no hostility toward him. Clearly, he enjoyed Jonathan, who was seductively stroking his puffy cheeks and alternately removing and replacing his glasses. "Your child is unusually friendly," he said to us, smiling. His remark pleased me.

However, recalling that moment now, I place beside it what Leon Wells, a death camp survivor and author of *The Janowska Road,* describes in his eyewitness account—how the SS would pick up children and smash their heads against a tree. These murderers were approximately the age of this German, who enjoyed the playfulness of our son Jonathan.

As the train lunged farther into Germany, Daniel continued to rock on my chest. In Paris, on our arrival at the station close to midnight, he had been almost too exhausted to walk to the train. Now he was sleeping fitfully within the darkness of the overheated coach. Meanwhile, the elderly man beside me had selfishly stretched out on his portion of the seat, jamming his leg, like a wedge, still further into my side.

But am I to complain of temporary discomfort when twenty years before, moving over those same tracks, the doomed, from within the fetid darkness of cattle cars, cried out for water. Twenty years before, they who were not to survive crouched beside corpses and excrement and whimpering children. . . .

In the morning, about eight, the train pulled into the main Nuremberg station. The Chairman of the English Seminar at the university had previously informed us by letter that, since he would then be on vacation in Switzerland, one of his student assistants would meet us at the station. So I had reason to expect that our arrival would be routine. Instead, what happened when the train halted was ugly, an outrage. A wedge of people waiting on the platform would not let us get off the coach. They hurtled up the steps and into the vestibule where we stood. They drove on as though they either did not see or were indifferent to the presence of our three children, who drew back, terrified.

The train would be leaving in five minutes—that much I made out from a voice over the loudspeaker system. Five minutes in which to get my family plus thirteen pieces of luggage off that train! Granted, such an incident could have occurred anywhere—France, Italy. But the difference is that it took place in Germany, and as we were attempting to step down on its soil for the first time.

Crude bestial faces and thick bodies drove toward us, pushed us aside, bowled into the coach. Frantic, enraged, I screamed for them to let us get off first. But they swept me aside. Where the hell are the conductors? I wondered, uselessly. If they trample my kids, I'll kill them.

I stood before my family with outspread hands, while a horde hurtled by either side of us. There must have been at least fifty of them. Someone slammed against my ribs. I barely checked an impulse to lash out with my fists. Whom, which one, would I have struck? Everyone who had ever pulled a Jew out of a transport car and beaten him mercilessly?

When the last one went by, I herded my family down the steps and onto the platform, then climbed back up into the vestibule, lowered thirteen pieces of baggage to my wife and cleared the train with only seconds to spare before it began moving.

So this is how we arrived. Welcome to Germany!

Guided by a young student assistant (he apparently had encountered some difficulty in identifying us), we left the station. Our first view was of castles and towers, remnants of the old city of Nuremberg. Darkly ominous they appeared to Tam and me, evoking images of medieval ghettos and torture chambers. In the near distance, thick walls looked sullenly at us, as if to say: What the hell are you Jews doing here? When Hitler lived we forced you to vacate your homes and leave the city until we were *judenrein*. Now what are *your* kind doing back here?

As we stood outside the station before a cab stand, Dina clutched a doll, her sole predictable and fixed connection to the severed past of San Francisco. Daniel held his stuffed teddy bear and Jon a cloth horse. All three kids looked dazed.

A large tree just outside the main entrance of the station was being cut down. Two men sliced into its trunk with an electric saw. Then the tree toppled and fell to the pavement with an enormous crash. Even now I can clearly see and hear the fall of that tree, how the roots came tearing out of the earth and lay strewn over the pavement; and I thought, It's like what has happened to us, after the rooted years in San Francisco. But now, please God, let there be no fall ahead of us, as the price for having come to Germany.

A cab large enough to contain all six of us plus baggage arrived, and then we were on the way to our new home.

The scenery from the cab windows? By then Tam and I were too emotionally drained to care. The young man from the Seminar kept up a well-intentioned running travelogue on Nuremberg while the kids elbowed each other, quarreling over who should sit where.

We drove past a castle, past walls, past gray, ponderous buildings, and finally came to a neighborhood of neatly cultivated vegetable gardens and gabled houses side by side under a gray sky. Under the roof of one such house the Baiers lived, the family from whom the English Seminar had, some weeks before, rented housing for us. The cab driver rang the front gate buzzer.

And so Frau Baier came into our lives. I can't recall her coming out of the house. In my memory the first time we see her, she is already standing at the front gate, waiting for us. She is dressed in a white apron, the hem of which her hands nervously crease and uncrease. Perhaps she wonders: What will this American family be like? Will she please them? And I wonder: Are we involuntarily linked in her mind with the American conquerors, whose Armed Forces brought the Third Reich to its knees? For she cannot have forgotten that American airplanes demolished entire sections of Nuremberg.

Has no one yet told her that there are Jews—yes, real live *Juden*—coming to live in her house? Because her obvious readiness to please appears entirely unqualified. Will she blanch when this fact becomes known to her? Will she tremble lest the neighbors hear?

Did I really entertain those thoughts on seeing her then, or am I now only first formulating them? Whatever the case, I am not entitled to a cheap portrayal of you, Frau Baier. You took us into your home and were good to my wife and children. When my wife became ill and took to bed for a week, you looked after her. My oldest son and daughter you taught how to ride a bicycle. Sleds you brought into the lives of all three. From you they came to know the lore of gardening. And in the summer, you bathed and sprinkled them with a hose as they sat rub-a-dub-dub all three in a large tin tub. (I still smile remembering the tub and the children, naked and singing, and you maneuvering the hose and laughing.)

But after the all-night journey and the incident at the station, we were not in a frame of mind to recognize your generous nature. Further, the discovery that neither you nor your husband spoke English, not a word, was traumatic. Also, at first glance, the part of the house which was to comprise our quarters appeared, to our eyes, conditioned by American suburban housing standards, confining and gloomy. The hall stairway going up to the second floor looked dangerously steep and high, and we immediately began worrying about the children. Tam was not happy about the kitchen gas stove, which was on the old-fashioned side. In sum, little annoyances, but they underscored the fact that the high-frequency adventures of our flight to New York, the sea voyage, and then the week in Paris had ended.

The young man from the English Seminar, having spoken with Frau Baier about our needs, relayed to her our questions about the operation of windows, doors, and locks and the location of public transportation and shopping facilities, and then took off, leaving us alone with the woman. And her with us. I wondered whether the young man (presuming he had gotten the information from his superior, who certainly would have looked at my Fulbright application, where the fact was clearly indicated) had informed her that we were Jews. . . .

From the first, it was apparent that she was aching to be of help to these helpless Americans who could not speak German. But despite her concern, a half hour after our arrival, Danny fell down a flight of stairs in the hallway. He had been descending from the second to the first floors. I bent over him, thinking, This is it—end trip. Broken back, casts, wheelchair, perhaps worse. (Later, Tam would tell me that when she saw Danny's body at the bottom of the stairs her first thought was—there it is. We've had it for coming to Germany.) But he stirred, was all right, wept. How he cried! And so, to help him get over the shock, I knelt and revengefully struck those goddamn steep stairs. Frau Baier grinned cautiously. Did she have some questions about how this American family was to fare under her roof?

Shortly after this mishap, little Jon complained—evidently had been doing so for some time until we finally heard him—that his shoes hurt him. In putting them on his feet, Tam had absently reversed their order. Suddenly she and I began to laugh. Our lives seemed like those shoes: left had become right, and right left.

Not that Frau Baier wasn't standing by to put on the shoes correctly. But the language she spoke was too threatening, too hopelessly incomprehensible; and in those first few hours after our arrival, we simply did not have the strength or patience to listen to it. Several days later I would begin to converse with the Baiers in a bizarre mélange of second-generation American-style Yiddish and horribly fractured German. But in the beginning, we kept her and the language at arm's length and stumbled around our quarters in whatever way possible.

That first day none of us left the house. What, pass beyond the front door and into the street! To where? To see whom? No one was waiting for us out there in Nuremberg, in this strange, disquieting place. That night, lying on an eiderdown bed, Tam and I half whispered, like conspirators. Directly below us, on the second floor, our landlords (briefly we had met Herr Baier earlier in the evening and had no clear impression of him other than that he seemed pleasant and hospitable enough) stirred. We heard voices. Were they speaking about the Americans, even as we were conversing about them? More pointedly, if they knew we were Jewish, had learned this through whoever it was at the university who had rented these accommodations, then couldn't we assume that the Baiers weren't Jew haters? But supposing they didn't have the slightest clue that Jews were lodged under their roof?

The unbroken silence of the streets below was disturbing. A silence as though we were shut up within castle walls, and no one would hear us if we had to cry out for help. . . .

I lay in the darkness, eyes wide, musing, my mind going back to that uprooted tree outside the train station, the roots pulled out of the earth, like entrails, leaving a hideous opening in the earth—like the gouged-out Jewish communities of Europe after the Nazis marched eastward.

In the morning we became even more aware that the glamour and exotica of travel had come to an end. Locks, heavy roll-up shutters, more locks, and varied sets of keys told us where we were. A less than modern stove and a backbreaking low sink told Tam where she was. There were two flights of a steep stairway between our rooms on the third and first floors that the children had to learn to navigate. On the morning of our second day Jon hadn't. He slipped, fell down several steps, adding bruised knees and elbows to bewilderment. I held a frightened, weeping three-year-old boy. In a word, the circumstances appeared *schlecht*.

What was going to be with our children? I wondered, borrowing parental worry. Where would they go to school? Who, if anyone, would become their friends? We had transported them some six thousand miles to this house and said: Now adjust. Make your own way. So, with the marvelous resilience of children, they would try. Still, what if in the days ahead they were reluctant to explore the neighborhood, to brave the obstacles of language, and continually stayed within the boundaries of the Baier home? The selfishness of parents! We—that is, I—wanted Travel, Adventure, Cause. But what was in it for them? What was Germany to them?

At which low point, shortly after Jon's fall, Frau Baier reappeared in our lives, bringing homemade cookies for Jon and a homespun Bavarian dress for Dina. She changed clothes; and then, behold the transformation of a five-year-old American girl into a *deutsches Mädchen!* Dina grinned, Frau Baier grinned; they were very aware of each other.

And now came the music—Sigi, the Baiers' twelve-year-old adopted son, and his accordion. At Frau Baier's insistence, he began by playing a Strauss waltz. He stood to one side of the first-floor living room; we sat on chairs. Well, not all of us. Dan and Dina jockeyed and elbowed each other, competing for a place on my lap, their father's lap which was, after all, reassuring anchorage as still another unfamiliar situation confronted them. Tam frowned because the kids, in competing for my lap, made the chair squeak. But Sigi appeared unperturbed. And leaning in the doorway, Frau Baier looked radiantly serene. What her presence and what the accordion said to us was: We realize you've come a long way, that you might be feeling at sea. So the music is to welcome you, to bid you be at home here.

A Proustian moment, then: Sigi, the accordion, Strauss, Frau Baier in the doorway, Rembrandtian light from the hallway moving softly over her shoulder, the children squirming in my lap—the incongruous images of history! In the concentration camps, accordionists in grotesquely striped uniforms played when the prisoners marched through the gates on the way to slave-labor assignments, and played again as they returned that evening, shuffling, stooped, caved in from fatigue, hunger, and harassment. And now, twenty years later, in Nuremberg, this German woman has brought her son to play music for us.

So a lovely half hour of music, and after Frau Baier left the room, obviously pleased by our applause, Dina, when Dan began wistfully reminiscing on his friends back in San Francisco, said, as though to sever some final connection to the past: "Let's forget about that. Let's see what new friends we will have here." Dina, who had walked down the *Queen Mary* gangplank at Cherbourg, holding aloft three red-and-orange balloons. *Voilà!* Our daughter arrives in Europe, smiling, floating balloons, as though supremely confident that no one would puncture them. *Voilà!*

I have already alluded to the tree outside the railroad station, and now there was another one, a medium-sized plum tree in the Baiers' backyard. It was early October and plums were falling, softly, as though from a perfect ripeness. In the windless air the branches of the tree were absolutely still. I listened and heard the sound of plums falling through the bright morning air to the ground. This tree, standing serenely against a peacock-blue sky, appeared to me like a promising sign, a benediction, of the year ahead. (Perhaps, in a similarly peaceful moment, Anne Frank had once written in her diary: "I don't think then of all the misery, but of the beauty that still remains. . . . My advice is: Go outside, to the fields, enjoy nature and the sunshine, go out and try to recapture happiness in yourself and in God. Think of all the beauty that's still left in and around you and be happy!")

A promising sign? But apprehension, nightmares, also. For on the second night, I, dreaming, saw Jon fall down a stairwell, from six flights up, and hit the ground floor with a hideous thud.

Leaning over a banister on the sixth floor, I heard his voice wailing. My God! Down the stairs I hurtled. His body was crumpled, but there was no blood. So perhaps he was still alive? I ran into the streets for a doctor, found one, and brought him back to the house. He knelt beside Jon's body. I wept hysterically. The doctor said that fortunately the body had been wrapped up in a wallet, which had padded the fall. But still, I thought, his body is much heavier than a wallet. So would he really live? And even if he did, at the lifelong price of a broken body, would we wish this for him?

Under the gabled roof, on a gray rainy morning of our third day in Nuremburg, I awoke in a proverbial cold sweat. Still shaken from the nightmare, I started out to see the city and its people. First I walked up and down the street on which the Baier house was situated. More gabled roofs, more windows shrouded by shutters, more heavy gates, immaculate sidewalks, immaculate lawns. Over the ledges of second- and third-floor windows sheets and eiderdown blankets were being aired out. A street of singular hygienic cleanliness.

A few acres of neatly arranged vegetable gardens were located a block from the Baier house. I walked along a country-like dirt road; and on both sides of it tidy gardens flowered. There I saw gardeners, men and women, on their hands and knees, caressing the soil. Gardeners of skill and thoroughness, they obviously care for earth and root and leaf. But had they cared as much for Jews?

In one plot of earth, just off to a side of the road, I saw an overturned, wheelless, rusting van. It was, I guessed, of a twenty-some-year-old vintage. The body was windowless, the inside lined with steel, and a double door in the rear might once have been hermetic. I remembered the vans that the Nazis had used, prior to the building of crematoria, for gassing their victims. Was this one of those vans? It did not occur to me then to pose the logical question that if by any chance such had once been the function of this van, what then was it doing here, in this place, rather than near one of the former death camps?

Why would it have been brought here? Pointless speculation this; still, from that time on, I could never pass that spot, pastoral though it was, without a sense of intense uneasiness.

From those gardens, I traveled to the center of the city, to the old town of narrow streets, defense towers, ruined walls, moats, stone bridges, gabled archways. A city whose beauty Hitler had compared to that of Florence. The people in the streets? Weary, hardened, and dour faces I saw, but of guilt, of remorse, not a sign. Their eyes appeared clouded, numbed, sightless. Survivors of the war who had all too soon become accustomed to eating well and buying homes, cars, luxury items.

Members of the former Jewish community of Nuremberg would have brightened this lusterless scene. Reportedly, that community had had ready wit, vivacity, and elegant style. They had helped give Nuremberg a reputation for cosmopolitanism and culture. Alas, in leaving the town during the Hitler years, they had left no mailing addresses.

But the anti-Semitic images of Jews were there, graven into the stone walls of churches and cathedrals—such as at St. Sebald. I stood there before a sculptured work that depicted a scene from Christ's stages of ascent. He was carrying the cross, and who should be behind him, hook- and sheep-nosed, dwarf-backed, treacherous, and rapacious, but some Fagin faces. Christ is going to Golgotha and his scourgers, the Jews—who else?—are immensely pleased. Mythology, then, for the masses—from medieval art to Belsen.

If on that first tour of Nuremberg, I did not see any of the former members of a distinguished Jewish community, neither did I see Brownshirt or SS thugs. Göring was not making a speech in a public square. The grotesque Julius Streicher was not striding through the streets in hobnailed boots and cracking his horsewhip.

And when I arrived at Zeppelin Wiese toward the close of that first day's touring, there too the recent past was dead. Weeds and bits of shrubs were growing in the ruined stands of the stadium, one of Hitler's monumental showplaces. I climbed up stone steps and came to the exact spot, the platform on which it is said Hitler stood while reviewing the marchers of the annual mass demonstration. Standing there, I pictured the banners, torches, martial music, formations, searchlights, klieg lights, columns of goose-stepping robots, thousands of uniformed arms raised in *Sieg Heil* to the rigid figure of the Leader, who promised German supremacy for a thousand years to come.

It was futile and senseless, this Cecil B. De Millesque exercise of the imagination. The might of the Third Reich had once passed this way, now all was ruins. In this place, I could not tangibly evoke the twelve black years nor find evidence of the deep-rooted anti-Semitism and xenophobia which, dating back to the Middle Ages, is said to be endemic of Nuremberg and the Franconian countryside.

So since the face of the recent past was invisible, I turned toward the present and those Germans closest to us.

2

SAGA OF THE VW

STARTING WITH FRAU BAIER.

From the very beginning she was ready to help us buy a car. Four or five miles separated her house from the location of a recommended car dealer, and she insisted we walk all the way. On principle and in practice, she was against streetcars and buses and would not use them as long as her legs or bicycle were functioning. So on the day of our long walk, she plunged ahead with explosive energy, head cocked forward and legs grinding like pistons, rapidly dissolving space; and I, who am considered by friends a demonic walker with Gulliverian strides, couldn't keep up with her. Where did she get such fantastic energy? What hearthstone-made bread had nurtured such sturdy bone and muscle? She strode forth like a Valkyrie to battle. Pavements trembled beneath her charge. With that same kind of indomitable energy she must have helped rebuild her house after the Allied bombings ended. Occasionally, she glanced back at me, almost apologetically, as though aware of my hard labor. In my memory, I see again the long plaited gray hair and girlish face of this fifty-some-year-old woman looking unbelievably young.

The dealer she brought me to didn't have a suitable used car for the amount of money I wished to spend, and so back we went to the house, again on foot, her whirlwind pace never faltering. I recall feeling footsore and bushed and saying to my wife, "Well, now I understand what's to account for the German economic miracle—thousands of Frau Baiers."

In that same week a car came to us. A service station manager in the neighborhood was the first person I spoke to on disembarking from a streetcar that had stopped near his place. On discovering that he spoke English, I asked for information on the way to the Baier house. Delighted that he could speak English, this discovery coming in the wake of a week's linguistic disasters between the Baiers and ourselves, I asked him whether he knew of a used car for sale. He did, indeed, and he was ready to show it to us the following day. "Wonderful," I said.

That's how our car troubles began—and persisted for the next six weeks. Persisted? Engulfed us—a nightmare. I'll not fully chronicle the events and persons in the saga of the car. What follows are a few selective vignettes to show how the jinxed VW introduced us to Germans of varied stations: Boger the service station manager, Hoff the mechanic, Koch the lawyer, and others.

I begin with Boger the service station manager: crew-cut, lackluster-eyed, late thirtyish, and looking like he hailed from the American Midwestern heartland. At first he was very accommodating in manner, and he sounded my name, Herr Halperin, as though he had silver bells in his mouth. "I like to see Americans happy," he said. Where had he learned English so well? In Brazil, after the war, he replied. Oh, yes, I thought, and checked the impulse to inquire what he was doing *there,* the haven of so many expatriate Nazis. And if he had been there, why had he returned? Then Boger introduced me to his business crony, a cold gray-eyed and boil-ridden man called Hoff, an auto mechanic. His nose and mouth were crooked, as though they had been placed on an anvil and hammered to one side.

And what was the car they removed from a used car lot in town? Hitler's car for the people: a funereal gray 1951 VW that I bought for 600 DM Plus extras, like a 100 DM wax and paint retouch job, which Boger convinced me was necessary. He himself volunteered to do this work, and I was readily agreeable.

(Later I would learn from a graduate student at the Seminar that I had easily overpaid two to three hundred marks for the car.)

All Americans have lots of money; you are American; therefore you expect to be overcharged. But I was annoyed that the car wasn't synchronized. To shift gears you had to double-clutch. No one had told us about that when we bought the car. I didn't even know what the lingo "double-clutch" meant; cars had never been my forte; in fact, until the age of thirty-five I was a perennial pedestrian. Anyway, the 1951 bugs were put together so that shifting was sheer hell, especially when you went from third to second and from second to first. Then the gear box screeched and the stick trembled, as though it were going to snap in two or be wrenched right out of the floorboard. No, the shifting wouldn't do for either Tam or me. As it is, we are nervous enough in traffic without having to worry about mechanical idiosyncrasies.

So the day after the purchase, I drove the car all the way in first gear to Boger's service station and poured out my complaint.

"Ah, troubles, troubles," he declaimed, as though he were addressing himself not to me but to the galleries of the universe. Hoff was summoned. He appeared and was adamantly opposed to returning our money. A concession? Well, if my wife and I were truly convinced that we couldn't master the procedure of double-clutching, he would synchronize the shifting. For a price, though, for another 600 DM.

So there it was (welcome to Germany!)—take the lemon and put it in *Ordnung* [order] or leave it. We took it. Hoff was commissioned to do the job. When Boger translated our decision to him, he smiled, and said, *"Jawohl."*

Was it a small victory for him? Did he gloat? For look here, the conquered had conquered the American conqueror. But the Jew? That he couldn't have known about then—the Jew within the American exterior. Because had he known, wouldn't he have claimed a double victory?

It was agreed that the car would be synchronized and returned to us within a week. "I told Hoff I'm going to kill him if he doesn't fix one hundred percent that damn car," Boger said, smiling, trying to be charming.

Frau Baier was furious. "That man cheated you," she said. By then that much in German I understood. "It's a bad car. Give it back to him. Come, I'll go to his place with you."

I argued for tact, forbearance, trust. After all, a guest in the land. She demurred, tentatively.

When the week was up, Frau Baier insisted on coming with me to pick up the car. Again she churned the sidewalk, head down, plunging ahead, her light-blue eyes flaring. She was readying for war.

Inside Hoff's garage, she burned her eyes into his cold ones and rat-a-tat-tatted in German. He snarled back. Turning to me, she said that he was a *schlechter Mensch*.

Hoff curtly pointed to the car and looked at me. *"Arbeit fertig* [the work is finished]," he said flatly, *"Prima, prima* [first class]."

I paid him the 600 DM, barely checking the impulse to say something sarcastic.

Frau Baier and I got into the car. As we drove out of the garage there was a horrible noise. A moment later I realized that the shift wouldn't stay in second gear, kept slipping out. Now something else was wrong.

Frau Baier observed my agitation. "Kaputt, no workee," I said to her, striking the wheel in anger. *"Schlechter Mensch, schlechter Mensch,"* she fumed. *"Er hat Sie angeschmiert* [he's cheated you]."

I didn't drive back to his garage. Because one look at that cold-eyed face of his and I would have been up for manslaughter. Instead, I drove directly to Boger's service station and told him the story. "Troubles, troubles, nothing but troubles from that bloody car," he whined. You would think that the financial burden was his. Clearly, too, I was no longer his favorite American, one that he liked seeing "happy." "Tell him to fix that car once and for all," I said, shouting.

"But, Mr. Halpereen, what can I do?" he continued to whine.

"What do I have to do with the whole bloody thing? I'm only one little man."

("What can I do? I was only one little man"—thousands of Germans thought when they saw Jews being beaten in public squares. "What can I do?" when they saw Jewish neighbors being forced to leave home for undesignated places. When the windows of Jewish-owned stores were smashed. "What could we do?" former Kapos, SS officers, and guards today plead in their own defense. "An order is an order. We did what we had to do. What could a little man do? We had only to say *Jawohl*.")

The clutch slippage was not the last of our troubles with that lemon. A few days after Boger returned it to me, the battery went stone-dead one morning. Luckily, I got a push from a smudge-faced chimney sweep, who wore a black top hat and hoops of wire around his shoulders, and so was able to drive on to Boger's station. We were stiffly hostile to each other. He said that the battery was shot. One could expect this to happen in an old car, he explained. "What now must be done?" I asked. He proposed the solution. So I let him sell me a new battery, and then we parted without a pretense at civility.

But now, though the car stayed in gear, the transmission made a terribly loud, piercing sound whenever I took my foot off the accelerator—like the pitiful groaning of a sick cow.

The owner of another service station in the neighborhood confirmed my suspicion. "Kaputt," he said of the transmission, shaking his head. He had a marvelously open smile, and you immediately felt you could trust him. A real *Mensch*.

His diagnosis clinched it, pushed me into deciding to get rid of the albatross. I asked him to keep me in mind if by chance he heard of anyone who might want to buy the VW. "*Jawohl, Herr Professor,*" he said cheerfully.

That evening I accidentally slammed a door of the car on our landlord's finger. What happened was that the left door wouldn't close all the way. Herr Baier happened to come by as I was opening and closing it, trying to locate the source of the trouble. He set out to help but apparently didn't seem to grasp the subtleties of what I wanted done, and since there was a sizable language barrier between us, I thought to demonstrate the problem graphically by once more opening and closing the door. What then happened was that somehow we got our signals crossed. I thought he had his hands out of the way. He screamed out.

Luckily, the finger wasn't broken but the poor man was in much pain. *"Macht nichts,"* he kept saying stoically, to reassure me. I felt awful. He took out a handkerchief and wrapped it around the finger. Then he looked at me with the most compassionate expression. The good man seemed more concerned about me than about his badly bruised finger.

A few days later, while fretting about the VW as it was proceeding through the intersection of a main street, I only partly glimpsed the black Mercedes bearing down at me. I slammed the brake pedal but the brakes (which were, as I later learned, defective) didn't grab. There was a shattering head-on collision, and the VW spun around and crashed into a curb.

Miraculously, I was not killed, not even injured, though the entire right side of the VW was caved in. Fortunately, also, the driver of the Mercedes, though stunned, was not even scratched. He apparently had applied enough braking power at the last moment so that the impact of the collision was largely checked. Still, the front end of his car was battered.

Clearly, it had been my fault. On coming to the main street, I obviously had continued through the intersection without first halting at the stop sign.

At once a ring of gaping spectators formed around the two cars. And curious faces appeared in the windows of the houses adjoining the intersection—faces that evoked images of the blank-faced spectators in the courtroom of Kafka's *The Trial.* They looked accusatory, those faces in the street and in the windows. I pictured them regaling one another in the spirit of unanimity about drunken, irresponsible American drivers. They looked at one another as if to say: "Isn't it terrible what those

Yanks have done to our country! Under Hitler we didn't have such nuisances." Yes, and with such gelid faces they must have looked on when elderly Jews were intimidated and beaten in the streets. And yet now they had the gall to say in stumbling, cloudy voices: We're not sure we saw anything. The past is all so hazy. . . . We can't remember.

I fumed. They accuse *me!* What right did they have to do so? If anything, I accused *them*—the murderers. *"Ich bin ein Yid."* Whimsically, I was tempted to cry out in J. F. Kennedy's *"Ich bin ein Berliner"* tone of voice. That would have jolted them. But instead, I remained standing by the side of the battered VW, assuming the absurd double burden of maintaining not only the image of personal dignity but also of American composure.

Presently the police arrived and promptly cited me for reckless driving; and then the battered VW and I were brought back by a tow truck to the Baier house.

I shall not dwell much longer on the saga of the VW. If I had the patience to detail still a few more incidents, I would relate how we finally sold the lemon and bought what turned out to be a very reliable 1953 VW from a customer of the honest service station owner, an old guy who sported a Kaiser Wilhelm mustache and stood sturdily and squarely on the ground. How the seller's wife, who reminded me of a favorite aunt, squeezed my hand warmly after we completed the deal, saying with moist eyes: *"Viel Glück. Wir haben Glück gehabt* [Much luck. We have had luck]." How I bought this car despite the warning of Frau Baier, who feared another lemon. *"Vorsicht, Vorsicht* [beware, beware]]," she grimly admonished. *"Glauben Sie mir!* [Believe me]. Why are you looking for more trouble?" she tried to tell me. Her advice was that we dispense with a car for the winter months and perhaps buy one in the spring. The streets will be icy soon, she added, and dangerous for driving. I reminded her of the job of getting the children to and from school, which was over a mile away. I'll take them on a sled, she offered with alacrity. "The sled is the best auto. *Billig und gut* [cheap and good]."

But her warning was not borne out by the sterling performance of the second VW throughout the rest of our stay in Germany. So that in time Frau Baier acknowledged I had chosen
well, philosophizing, *"Nach dem Schlecht, kommt das Gute*
[After the bad, comes the good]."

And how, since I considered suing Hoff, a German lawyer
came into our lives. Enter Koch with a sporty silk scarf, close-
cropped hair, steel-blue eyes, a patrician nose—altogether a
highly photogenic Tyrone Power type. "Professor Halperin," he
said several minutes after we had met, "try to forget what Hitler
did to the Jews," which, curiously, he pronounced Yoos. "And
please don't have a bad impression of Germany because of this
one bad mechanic." He talked a lot about Hitler. "Hitler lied to
us. I myself realized this when I was serving on the Russian
front, but by then it was too late to do anything about it. But
Hitler wasn't the only one who lied to us. Your F.D.R. did too.
So did Churchill. But mainly F.D.R. He promised our diplo-
mats he wouldn't oppose us if we attacked the Bolshevists. And
then he went back on his word. He destroyed Dresden. We
wanted to be friends with the U.S. You were always our friends.
Anyway, please don't believe we're still the same people we
were under Hitler. We're changed now. We're a new Germany.
Believe this."

And for the coda there was one last encounter with Hoff
when we glared at each other, eyeball to eyeball, and I had to
suppress the impulse to smash his face. Koch had strongly advised against my using any violence if I was planning to take
him to court. So I settled for telling him what I thought of the
car he had sold me. I think he got the message. Then I tore out
of the garage. Perhaps worried that I might be planning to sue
him, he ran after me, clumsily attempting to be civil, concilia-
tory. So I had a bone of satisfaction by not replying and keeping
my back turned on him as I went out of his life, bringing to an
end (excepting some subsequent minor legal hassles with the
law over my admitted guilt in the accident) six weeks of trouble
from that lousy VW.

I have touched on this trivial business with the car to show

how badly I initially carried on in Germany. Perhaps I ought to have punched Hoff—the hell with the lawyer's advice. As it was, despite all my reading on the Holocaust, despite all that I thought I had learned from long reflecting on it, my conduct, ironically, had been that of a *victim*.

3

WHAT I MIGHT HAVE DONE...

KAFKA-LIKE FANTASIES of what I should have done and didn't . . .

Why didn't I shout out into the face of the conductor aboard the train between Nuremberg and Erlangen, *"Ich bin ein Yid"*? A conductor, a middle-aged German with what poisoned past during the Hitler years? A longtime employee of German railroads, I would wager, so perhaps he was once commended for his part in the efficient operation of deportation trains. Now, twenty years later, this conductor was aboard a train running between Nuremberg and Erlangen, where I taught classes in American literature at the university. Thick-faced and knob-eared, gimlet-eyed and sharp-nosed, he grumbled and punched my ticket and made it abundantly clear that my Americanized German displeased him. So on that day when he was exceedingly curt in answering my question about the procedure for getting a refund on an unused ticket, shouldn't I have hurled the words right into his ears and watched him recoil? I can imagine his face freezing, then crumbling, piece by piece. And if he became abusive, I could have gotten up and pushed him out of the way. From him, in 1964, I didn't have to take anti-Semitic insult.

Another fantasy: I could have sounded off against the white-haired, arrogant-faced elderly lady at the outdoor restaurant. I recall how she sat down beside me at the only available table, without so much as a perfunctory acknowledgment of my presence. At once she pushed an empty soup bowl, which had not yet been cleared away by the waitress, out of her way and toward me. Her fingertips—for it was with them alone that she deigned to move the bowl—and face expressed absolute aversion for the object. There was no semblance of humanity on her face, none. A face not unlike those in the photographs of captured women guards at Buchenwald.

When finally the order of *Bratwürste* arrived, I sidelong watched her eating with an expression of detestable hauteur. Exactly at the moment when a shred of meat was wriggling like an eel between her teeth I might have spoken the words, leaning forward for emphasis—*"Ich bin ein Yid."*

Her bloodless eyes would have blinked, as though a foreign body had lodged in them. I imagine her fork hesitating in midair but her eyes still avoiding my face, as if she hadn't heard. Then the ascent and descent of her fork and knife would resume, but now much more slowly, as though her appetite had been blunted. I would pay the waitress and leave without proffering the customary *Auf Wiedersehen* to the woman, thereby hoping that my impoliteness had offended her.

I could extend the list of should-have-dones to the perpetually dour-looking retired doctor whose house bordered the Baiers'. In all the months we lived there he never once raised up his eyes to say hello to us, never once gave us a single sign of common civility. Why? The Baiers once or twice made some reference to his being a decent, friendly gentleman. Well, then, why so bellicose-looking whenever we saw him? Had someone —the mailman perhaps (since we regularly received letters from Israel)—told him that we might be Jews? Or, more simply, was he down on all Americans because of what may have happened to him in the war?

So trivial a thing, really. A man appears to be unfriendly, so why make a big production of it? Yet, I would remember the medical doctors in the Nazi extermination camps, the prisoners they murdered, corpses they dissected, skulls they embalmed.

Could he have been one of these killers? But even supposing we had known this to be the case, then what? Would we have gone into his house and accused him? Would we have taken him bound to a tower of the Old City and there, before the eyes of the populace, hanged him as prisoners were hanged in the camps?

But why all this blather, then, over a man who may have been as benign as Alyosha Karamazov? I'm not sure. Perhaps to illustrate how such subjective arithmetic for a Jewish visitor in post-Auschwitz Germany might well add up to faulty sum totals.

4

REPENTANT GERMANS?

THE PROGRAM WAS ADVERTISED as *Der Rabbi singt*. It
was held in the student union of the university, and the auditorium was filled, mostly with young people. The singers were
young German students from Berlin. They apparently had pre-
sented the same concert at other German universities. We did
not know whether they were Jewish or not, but to Tam's ears
and mine their Yiddish sounded authentic enough. It is difficult
to say how much the audience understood. Before each number
an announcer spoke a few words in German; and the program
notes, which had been distributed earlier, should have helped il-
luminate the songs' content. Whatever the case, the audience
apparently grasped enough to be visibly moved. What the singers and what the audience response seemed to communicate is
this: a gifted people, and now, tragically, they are gone.

It was eerie. Germans singing Jewish folk songs. But where
were the Jews? Were Tam and I the only ones there, in vir-
tually *judenrein* Erlangen? Really, it was as though the songs
might have been those of a vanished race. Granted, the audience
felt sentiment and sorrow for the departed. But it was probably
too easy for it to do so—like nostalgia over the passing of the
good ol' darkies of the plantation days. After the songs died
away and the listeners left the auditorium and went home to their
parents, what did these young people say to them? Dear parents,
where were you when Jews were being murdered?

In retrospect, I do not overvalue the weeping of that audience. How much did it cost them, after all, to feel sorrow for a vanished people? By comparison, I think now of a children's program witnessed in Vilna during March of 1942 by Herman Kruk, former director of the Grosser Library in Vilna who died in a Nazi extermination center. He described this event in his diary (*Diary of the Vilna Ghetto,* pp. 27–28; YIHO Institute for Jewish Research, 1961):

> For a long time I have not experienced such a sensation. Hundreds of children . . . singing . . . and the audience responding with weeping. Across the width of the stage stretches a pipe, leading to a small stove. This is the only source of heat in the auditorium. The children crowd around the pipe. A mother sits and weeps. I know her. She weeps over her child left with a Christian family. Another one weeps because her sister and brother were taken to Ponary. And is there one here that has nothing to weep for? On the stage there is a rink. The children use their imagination. There are no rinks in the ghetto so they have made one of the stage. The children skate, move their feet to the rhythm of the music . . . and create the illusion.

Less than a week from that particular performance, Vilna would be heavily bombed and many in the audience would die.

All were attired in black and they moved slowly along the highway toward the town cemetery. We would learn it was the day of the year on which Germany mourns the war dead. There were perhaps five hundred of them. They moved as though they were in great pain.

My family and I sat in our car, waiting for them to pass so that we could continue along the highway. Tourists in search of castles and churches, we were on our way from Nuremberg for a day's outing in the country.

Stony-faced, with lowered heads and numbed faces, the mourners walked close to one another, as though they had been seared by a common grief. I did not think then, not even cas-

ually, of the millions of Germans dead from the war. Nor did I
feel pity. What for? For the followers of Hitler? *Who,* after all,
had started the war? *Who* had established the ghettos, the concentration camps? *Whose* countries had been occupied, shack-
led, starved?

What did our children make of the mourners and their parents' response to them? I'm not sure. Certainly we didn't make
it an occasion for a story on the "bad man" Hitler. What should
we have told them? That ordinary Germans, looking not unlike
the Baiers, who were being so kind to them, had killed Jews,
had destroyed cities, turned Europe into mass pyres? Should we
have told them that it was hundreds of people looking not unlike the Baiers who were now walking along the highway toward
the cemetery?

So Tam and I waited in silence for the black-clad figures to
pass by. Even so, Dina apparently sensed something, because
she said, with a troubled expression, "Daddy, let's go."

Finally the mourners cleared the highway and slowly went
on. In my memory now, silent and ponderous, they are still
moving along that road toward the cemetery.

But if a strong man, in the image of the Führer, again arose,
would they not follow him? Have they really learned a lesson?
Are they really free of their attraction to strong men? Because
look how Germans carried on at the death of Kennedy. Thousands of mourners in the streets, marching in midnight torchlight convocations, and all night condolence calls to the American Embassy in Berlin. A massive outpouring of tears, regrets,
eulogies. Why so excessive? Tam and I had wondered. He
wasn't, after all, *their* president. Because Kennedy had said, *"Ich
bin ein Berliner"*? Because Kennedy was the youthful, energetic
image of a valuable ally, the United States, the country which
had stood Germany back on its economic feet after the war?
Because he was the personified image of the Hero? Did they
sense that here was another Leader? He would speak and they
would pick up arms and march. Against whom? Against the
Russians one day, Chinese the next. They would march on willfully, blindly, at the behest of a strong voice. Only that. Because

try to picture them weeping if that gentle man Adlai Stevenson
had been shot down. No, then they would not have stood in the
public squares and wept. Not for a gentle man who could laugh
at himself. Not for a man who was immune from a grandiose
sense of himself as being heavy with Destiny. *"Ich bin ein
Berliner."* Let the Russians hear and beware. Clank of armor,
rumble of guns, explosion of human bodies. Kennedy spoke and
the pulse of postwar Germans—apparently even of the younger
internationalist-minded, antinationalistic, generation—fluttered.
And if he had asked them to march over The Wall, would they
have done so? Seeing the tensed, set jaws of men and women as
they stood in the public squares of Nuremberg, listening to
speakers eulogize Kennedy, watching the torchlight processions
of college students, the populace crowding the local Amerika
Haus, determined to register their names and sentiments in condolence ledgers, I could not help feeling that their emotions
leaped out toward what they sensed had been the mailed fist in
the martyred president. For him would they have been ready to
die—as they had been for the Führer?

I come now to the day the Baiers learned that the American
family living under their roof was Jewish. Until that point they
apparently hadn't known this about us. Not even our speaking
in lame Yiddish gave them a clue. "You speak a funny
German," Frau Baier once said to us, looking amused, puzzled.
"It's like Old Testament Deutsch—the way Adam and Eve
talked."

One day when I was teaching in Erlangen and the Baiers had
Tam over for a cup of late afternoon coffee, they were shocked
on hearing her disclose who we were. This is the story, as I later
learned it from her. The conversation turned around to the
coming Christmas. The Baiers were already planning for it.
How were we going to celebrate? Frau Baier asked, in all apparent innocence. At first Tam tried to be elusive, feigned not to
grasp the drift of their question. "Are you Catholic?" Frau
Baier asked. "No, we're not Catholic," Tam replied. Why Catholic? Apparently Tam's dark complexion, and that of Jon's and

Dina's also, had led them to suppose that we might be of Italian descent. And for them to be Italian was automatically to be Catholic.

"Nicht katholisch," Frau Baier said hesitantly. *"Dann protestantisch?"*

"Nein, nicht Protestant."

So then I can imagine the awkward silence, the puzzlement on the faces of the Baiers. Because if one wasn't either Catholic or Protestant, then *what* could one possibly be?

Tam said Frau Baier looked quizzically at her husband, he looked at her.

"So next she asked," Tam related, " 'Then what?' I meant to answer 'Jewish.' But probably if I had said this in English, they would not have known the word. So instead I said, *'Ich bin ein Yid.'* It was, as I later discovered, a terrible blunder. They had every reason to be stunned. *Yid* in German would be for them equivalent to someone here saying 'kike' or 'sheeney.' Or like using 'nigger' for 'Negro.' I should have said, *'Ich bin ein Jude.'* I know this now. But in that moment, given my awful Yiddish-Deutsch, I didn't know how else to answer.

"You can imagine what my disclosure did to them. An American family comes to live under your roof. Nobody forewarns you that they're not just Americans. You perhaps brag to the neighborhood about your renters, because Americans in Germany are, at least this year, 'in.' And this is a Herr Professor family to boot. Then, without warning, here's this American woman saying that she's Jewish!

" 'And is your husband Jewish also?' Herr Baier asked in an incredulous tone. He did not look pleased. 'Yes,' I said flatly.

"They looked as though they had had it. He in particular couldn't hide what he felt, a tight knot of distress showing in his expression.

"Frau Baier was the first to speak. 'We are all brothers,' she said. In such an awkward moment it was the diplomatic thing to say. But, unmistakably, she was shaken, and Herr Baier even more visibly so. He could hardly meet my eyes. Then, as though to dissociate themselves from the recent past, Frau Baier said, quietly, that the Jews didn't have it good under Hitler. So they went away, disappeared.

"Can you imagine! They voluntarily *went away*. She said this in all seriousness, with a completely guileless expression, and added that the *Krieg* was *schlecht*, as though no one had ever told her *how* Jews had disappeared up the chimneys.

"Then, to make matters even more awkward, Sigi, who had been in the room all the while, asked them, 'What is a Yid?' [Sigi, an extremely shy, reticent boy, rarely asked questions of his parents—at least in our presence.] You should have seen their faces hearing *that* word again. They curtly told Sigi they would speak to him later. I only hope that if they explained to him what a Yid is, they also got around to explaining *why* it was that the Jews *went* away from Nuremberg."

"Well," I said, "after today it'll be interesting to see whether they're still warmly hospitable."

They were—at least on the surface. Did they tell themselves —well, these are not like the Jews who once lived here? From America, after all, and especially a Herr Professor and his family. Or maybe they honestly felt the spirit of brotherhood. I didn't know then—and maybe it's for the best that we remained in the dark. Because supposing we knew for certain that, out of our hearing, they execrated us as Jews? Or supposing we knew for certain that the Baiers had been among those who broke the windows of Jewish stores on Crystal Night, who cheered when Hitler cried, "Down with the Jews!" and rejoiced when the synagogues were burned down? Would we then, on the basis of such knowledge, have been prepared to move, to uproot the children again, to wrench them away from *their* Frau Baier, to undergo the many inconveniences of changing quarters? Not very likely. Nevertheless, for a time after that incident I sometimes wondered—most probably without warrant—whether the Baiers were scrutinizing our physiology and conduct for traits resembling the grotesquely caricatured Jews of *Der Stürmer*.

5

THE YOUNGER GENERATION

LOOKING BACK, I see that this incident concluded the first phase of our stay in Germany. We had been in Nuremberg six weeks. It had taken us that long to get the children settled at a nearby school for dependents of U.S. armed services personnel, find a dependable car, get accustomed to traveling around Nuremberg, and become less intimidated by the sound of German. Only then did we feel ready to venture away from the boundaries of the Baier home.

And so we came to know some members of an English-speaking discussion group which met one evening a week at the Amerika Haus. The objective of the membership was to get practice in conversational English. What got discussed were such topics as German education, the civil rights movement in the United States, American progressive education, contemporary American writers, and so on. At each meeting, someone would present a prepared talk and afterward there would be questions from the others, who usually constituted some thirty to fifty in number. The members were generally in their late twenties and early thirties, and they tended to be white-collar workers, students, translators, engineers, chemists, elementary and secondary school teachers. One of the Amerika Haus librarians undertook the job of leading the group. She was especially eager to invite Americans living in the area to participate in the meetings. On learning of my presence as a lecturer at the university, she sent me a special invitation.

Among those who frequently attended the meetings were two American girls. One worked as a secretary for a Nuremberg business firm (on weekends and holidays she often traveled in Europe), and the other girl was employed by the American Army, in one of the civilian service departments of the local military command. Both were native New Yorkers. The girls, whom I shall refer to as Diana and Kay, knew a number of the group's members well enough to have been invited for dinner to their homes; and they graciously saw to it that Tam and I were "circulated" around.

We are especially grateful to them for having introduced us to two impressive young men, Rolf and Gunther. During our stay in Nuremberg, Tam and I saw a great deal of them and the two American girls. There were some pleasant parties in one of the girls' apartments or in our place, and the six of us went on some enjoyable country outings. Or we would sit in a Nuremberg *Gasthaus* around a large wooden table, drinking beer and wine and chatting amiably. None of the four appeared in the least surprised when, on one occasion, several weeks after meeting them, we casually revealed our Jewish identities.

In time, the young men began to speak of the recent past. We heard how it was for them during the Hitler years, Allied bombings, the first postwar years of unheated classrooms and stringent food rationing. They candidly stated their opinions on such questions as reparations to the Jewish people and the teaching of the history of National Socialism and the Third Reich in German schools. What they had to say on these matters—and they expressed themselves in excellent English—paralleled what we later were to hear from other members of the discussion group and from some of my students at the university. They felt that Germans must make just restitution for what was done to European Jewry. But at the same time they resented the efforts of many people, both inside and outside Germany, to make them feel guilty about the Nazi crimes.

Perhaps both of them had earned the right to feel vexed on this count, because they were evidently doing their best to face up to the German crimes of the recent past. Rolf, for one, had

written and produced a radio skit which reminded listeners that
it was precisely during the Christmas holidays when stores
owned by Jews had been vandalized. And Gunther was a severe
critic of present-day university student dueling societies, their at-
tendant ultrareactionary values and pernicious pseudopatriotic
practices. Altogether, both young men were intelligent, independ-
ent of mind, tough-willed, outspoken.

We, nevertheless, found unconvincing Gunther's statement
that, in his memory, Nuremberg Jews had never been—not even
in the days of Hitler—physically abused in public. True, he admitted that they were forced to wear the yellow star and sit in
separate places aboard streetcars. "In school we were told they
were to blame for everything. But no one ever struck at them,"
Gunther said. "In Nuremberg they were not told where they had
to live. My parents and many of their friends thought of the
Jewish people as fellow neighbors and citizens. Then they
started to disappear—sometimes overnight. We asked our parents where so and so went to and were told that they went to
live in another city. Our parents actually believed this was the
case. It is true that in those days Jews were being rounded up
and marched to the railroad station. But none of the Germans
escorting them was carrying a gun. So we all thought they simply were on their way to work in other parts of Germany. This
is what we were told. Actually, we thought more about the German prisoners of war in Russia—how they were dying of star-
vation. Each one had his own problems then. You worried only
for your family and your friends.

"Then we began hearing rumors of mass shootings in the
East. We didn't believe these stories could be true. And even if
we had reason to doubt them, what could we have done about
it? You protested and you were shot. How many of us are such
big heroes? Nazi party members were on the alert for anyone
who made unpatriotic remarks. You were not supposed to read
the leaflets that Allied planes dropped in the night, leaflets ad-
vising the Nuremberg population to prepare for occupation and
to avoid resistance against the American soldiers.

"I remember picking up one of them from the streets and going with a friend into a sandpile. We pulled a blanket over our heads and, in semidarkness, we read it. Each of us was twelve years old, and we felt we were being heroic. Later, when we told our parents, they were shocked, furious. 'Don't ever do that again!' they ordered us.

"So if you were not supposed to make comments against the Third Reich, how much more dangerous it would be to interfere with what was, on the surface, the peaceful exodus of your Jewish neighbors. Because as I say, they went to the railroad station and no mob was running after them, cursing or throwing stones, as they did in Poland, Hungary, elsewhere.

"The point is we want the world to understand what happened here not in order to *forgive* us but to realize how these things could have happened. How step by step the population was silenced, repressed.

"Granted, we were cowardly, but it really angers us when we learn about the stupid TV programs in the States showing moustached Germans looking treacherous and brandishing truncheons. And we have seen the science fiction books and detective books on *bad* Germans.

"This is not us!" Here Gunther's voice registered a sense of outrage. "Won't they see us as we really are? Finally it comes to a point when you say to yourself about visitors from abroad who have come here prepared to accuse—go to hell your own way! Just leave me alone. I just can't be bothered, can't go on indefinitely feeling guilty, apologetic. . . ."

I could well understand why Gunther should speak to us on this matter. He knew of my interest in the history and literature of the Holocaust. Understandably, Rolf and he must have wondered whether I had come to Germany not as an impartial, open-minded observer but rather, as Gunther put it, in order to accuse, to judge.

At any rate, it seemed to Tam and me that they had earned the right to speak out now. Earned it because, during the war and the early postwar years, they had experienced hard times.

They had especially earned the right to speak out because they were actively working for a democratic Germany.

Still, after hearing them out, we had two distinct reservations. First, it seemed to us there was an undercurrent of self-pity in some of what they said. Later, we were to detect this same tone in other members of the discussion group and also among my students at the university, even though we could understand that they felt unjustifiedly picked upon for being descendants of the older generation.

And yet I thought: Don't they share the guilt? Aren't they also guilty? For a nation doesn't live only in the present; it also lives in a continuum across the generations. So they ought not to argue that what happened in the past has nothing to do with them. Instead, isn't it their responsibility to share—and without self-pity—the hard burdens of making due restitution?

As to Gunther's claim that Nurembergers did not know what was happening to the Jews, we couldn't believe that. They *knew* —at least in substance if not in detail. They had seen or heard that Jews were leaving the city and yet they had neither the courage nor moral imagination to ask questions about where they were going. Nor can I believe that no Jews were ever beaten in the public streets of Nuremberg.

Maybe Gunther never saw such beatings but others in the discussion group did. I have in mind a story told to me by a young man. One evening in the early '40s, his father, on coming home from work, slumped into a chair and began weeping. Earlier in the day he had stood by watching while one of his dear neighbors, a Jew, was being beaten by a policeman in one of the city's main public squares and before a crowd of jeering spectators. "What could I do?" this young man's father kept saying over and over again. "If I had tried to interfere, they would have put me in jail. If I had tried to say something, the police would have ordered me to move on." It was as though he were asking his family to acquit him. "So what should I have said to my father?" the young man asked of me, as though, twenty years later, I was expected to render judgment. "What should I have said to him?" he repeated, and the question seemed to echo in the air.

Across the way, on one side of the sloping cobblestone square, is the Albrecht Dürer house. We—Rolf, Gunther, Tam, and I—sit in an outdoor café located on the opposite side of the square. The highest and most imposing structure in this setting is the Tiergärtnertor, one of the five principal tower gates of old Nuremberg. Built in the thirteenth century, this massive tower of stone is about 130 feet high and has a thickness of some 16 feet and a diameter of 59 feet. The corners of its upper two floors contain the familiar stone oriel windows (decorated corner turrets), which in earlier centuries were so typical of Nuremberg architecture. Three quarters of the way up on the tower's facade is the carved image of an eagle, the traditional coat-of-arms insignia for the historical city of Nuremberg. Branching off from each side of this edifice is a narrow wooden passageway where soldiers once stood on the lookout for any possible hostile force. The passageway is part of the elaborate ring of tower walls and fortifications that made the town impregnable. To one side of the tower is the gateway to the winding tunnel through which wayfarers over the centuries have entered and left the old city.

Directly to one side of the Tiergärtnertor is the half-timbered Pilatus house, on one side of which we are sitting. Attached to the front of this dwelling is the life-size figure of a knight in armor that once served to indicate the trade of the harness maker Grünenwald, who had his shop there in the fifteenth century. Looking up and high over the top of the Pilatus house, we see the monumental Kaiserburg, the castle that Hitler viewed as a symbol of Teutonic fighting courage. As our eyes move farther around the square, they rest for a moment on the venerable restaurant, the long half-timbered Gasthaus Schranke, which was built around 1500.

Then our eyes come back to one of the most famous buildings in the world, the Dürer House. Its first two stories are made of sandstone ashlar; and the next two stories have horizontal beams at the floor levels and windowsills and uprights braced by diagonals. Erected around 1450, it is the only completely preserved Gothic burgher house in Nuremberg. Sandstone lower stories and half-timbered upper ones, wide windows and a wooden balcony, truncated gable and gabled dormer, the house rises up from the corner of the square "a thing of beauty . . . forever." It is fitting that in such a dwelling the great Dürer had worked. From his windows he could see overhead the strongholds and towers of the Kaiserburg. Or he might look down at the cobblestone square over which the citizens of Nuremberg (there were only 25,000 inhabitants at that time) would be moving slowly. In such a time, with the Tiergartnertor encircling the street on which he lived, creating an atmosphere of security and containment, Dürer must have felt encouraged to do his best work, some of which is now displayed inside the house. There one finds watercolors of animals, birds, grass and herbs, drawings of dancing peasants with thick legs and sturdy hips, studies of children's heads and of hands in prayer, scenes of Nuremberg courtyards, the Pegnitz River, portraits of knights on horses or leaning on lances, patrician ladies and elegantly attired noblemen, elderly ladies in marketplaces, firewood strapped to their backs and dead roosters hanging from their waists and selling potatoes from straw baskets, the kneeling saint greeting a stag in the engraving *St. Eustace,* the terrifying figure of Death barring the way of the heroic knight in the copper plate, *Knight, Death, and Devil,* and a reproduction of the magnificent *Adam and Eve.*

But on this afternoon, the four of us do not feel the need to look again at the Dürer collection in the house; we are content to sit under the sun in the outdoor café, leisurely conversing and enjoying the setting. Rolf and Gunther speak of Nuremberg's past. Where do they get it from, their detailed and extensive historical knowledge? I especially envy the sense of authority with which they speak of themselves as Europeans. To be brought up in Europe, I daydream, to speak more than one language. To be able to reach back with familiarity into your national history, century upon century, tradition upon tradition. Not to be the perennial all-American freeway boy but rather to sit still, expostulating with taste and intelligence on literature, art, music. They speak about European history and culture, and one practically *sees* the presence of kings and nobility, the color and pageantry of tournaments and masked balls.

Still, there's a historical irony here. Centuries earlier than the Germans, the Jews were a community, a cohesive people. In Canaan they lived concretely, in touch with place, with earth. Their days were thick, not yet thinned out from centuries of wandering and dispersement as history's number one running people. In Canaan their history cohered and was closely webbed. It was *they* who were the chroniclers of history.

And now, thousands of years later, the situation is turned around as Tam and I sit in Tiergärtnertor Square with Rolf and Gunther. It is their rooted ancestors who have laid claim to the same ground for centuries while we have been the travelers, the dispossessed. Having been driven away from the land of churches and castles, it is we who must now hear about European history from the descendants of "rooted" Germans.

But we once lived in Germany, too, I could have said, in all accuracy, to our two companions. In the fifteenth century the Halperins—I learned this only recently—lived in Heilbronn, a town on the Neckar, some thirty miles north of Stuttgart and one of the key stops on the well-known Burgenstrasse which transverses Mannheim, Heidelberg, Heilbronn, Rothenburg, and Nuremberg. So I might have been born in Germany had my great ancestors been allowed to live there in peace. But instead the road of exiles that led to Spain and France and Germany went on to Romania, Poland, Russia. If not for the wandering, perhaps Rolf, Gunther, and I might have been conversing out of a common national and cultural heritage.

But looking back now, as I muse on this if-if track of history and circumstances, private and collective, the thought occurs to me that if the road had not opened to the East and the Halperins had stayed in Germany, would Tam and I have been sitting there? Had the road not gone to Russia and then westward to the New World, it probably would have been our turn, some twenty years before, to have entered a gas chamber. And before that final moment, we would have had occasion, as German Jews, to observe how the generation of Rolf's and Gunther's parents smashed the windows of Jewish shops and houses and razed synagogues. (Perhaps Rolf and Gunther and we would have met here, in Nuremberg, and what would they have had to say to us when, by their own admission, they were then members of Hitler's youth movement?) And yet there we were, sitting in the sun beside the Tiergärtnertor, conversing on German history and culture!

Because the road ran from Germany to Eastern Europe and then westward to the New World—New York, Chicago, San Francisco, I am a baseball buff but know nothing about soccer, can speak knowledgeably of skyscrapers and subways, and know very little about castles and cathedrals. I lack Rolf's and Gunther's social grace, from the ordering of a meal to the ways in which they can discuss, say, a painting. My conversation gives itself away from the outset, contains little mystery; whereas theirs is oblique, full of bends and surprises, like European streets. When they speak about traditions, the word *immer* is often on their lips. And they seem to have learned some sense of control and circumspect disinterestedness. Faustian hungers there are in all men, but Rolf and Gunther seem to have resisted or at least proportioned them. They have been spared the American nervous tic of lunging restlessly and centrifugally and wastefully through geographical space.

Still, cultural and national differences aside, there is something about the setting, our companions, that seems familiar— as though we had all been friends and contemporaries in another age somewhere on the Continent. Their company makes us feel—I do not know how else to express this—European. It is as though we are resuming a relationship that had been of long standing before the road went to the New World. One sits and leisurely converses, drinks tea, nibbles on pastries, and the atmosphere is warmly communal, strangely familiar. . . .

Noting that I had published several articles on Thomas Wolfe in college and general publications, one of the English Seminar professors invited me to teach a seminar on Wolfe. This course offering made sense to me in that Wolfe, who was of American-German descent, had written on his experiences in pre-World War II Germany, and the adventures of his protagonists resembled those of Goethe's Werther and sometimes of a young Faustus.

So then several tall, Wolfe- (who had been nearly six feet five) high, graduate students and I met twice a week. Since I stand almost six feet three, I am not undersized; and yet in their collective presence I often felt dwarfed. Coming and going as a group, we must have formed an arresting picture. It is one that would have amused Tom Wolfe; he would have recognized the comic in a roomful of German Gullivers "studying" his mammoth-sized books.

They were bright, articulate, and exceptionally motivated students, and their spoken and written English was impressive. I especially admired—and as a monolinguist felt intimidated by —their mastery of three or more languages. Why were they taking the course? Partly, to be sure, because a certain number of course units in seminars were required of graduate students. But, also, because they had a genuine interest in American literature, and some planned to go to American universities for advanced graduate study in English and American literatures.

What did they know about Wolfe? Not very much, really. The usual information. That he had traveled in and written on the Germany of the '30s; and that frequently he had been referred to as the American Homer. Yet none of the students had recently read any of the novels.

In my introductory remarks, I discussed his love for Germany. How in comparison with it, he found other European countries pallid. Holland, for example, he found too small and

its people too staid. England struck him as filled with inert, quietly despairing people. Paris for George Webber, one of Wolfe's
autobiographical protagonists, had the "smell of dead air,
used-up, tainted oxygen . . . the smell of millions of weary and
unwashed people [here the students laughed, as though out of a
wry, cosmopolitan sense of familiarity with Parisian life] who
had come and gone and breathed the air and used it up and left
it there—dead, stagnant. . . ." Venice for him was the place
of "suspended sewage floating in old walls." How badly it
compared, Webber observed, with cities like Rothenburg and
Nuremberg. How could, say, Marseilles, with its "tainted odor
of the South," compare with the "excellent life" of Berlin or
the "clean smell . . . and almost odorless odor" of Munich?
About Munich he was especially exuberant. Speaking of that
city, George Webber said, "Some people sleep and dream they
are in Paradise, but all over Germany people sometimes dream
they have come to Munich." Altogether, Wolfe did not see how
anyone who came to Germany, as he once wrote to his editor-
friend, Maxwell Perkins, "could possibly fail to love this
country, its noble Gothic beauty and its lyrical loveliness, or to
like the German people who are, I think, the cleanest, the
kindest, the warmest-hearted, and the most honorable people
I have met in Europe."

Laughter and chuckles from the students in response to such
unqualified enthusiasm for Germany and Germans. I liked their
sense of irony. So "unpatriotic" a response in an age of venom-
ous nationalism seemed a healthy sign.

They seemed similarly amused in reading of Wolfe's fierce
hungers of the belly and mind: his hunger for the varieties of
cheeses, roasts of meat, smoked hams, sausages, fine wine and
beer, and the "delicious miracles" of pastry in the stores of
Germany; and the Faustian hunger in him for art museums and
especially bookshops, with their "swarming multitude of Gothic
print, that staggering superflux of German culture which sad-
dened him with an intolerable and impossible hunger for posses-
sion." Some students knowingly nodded their heads when I re-

marked that sometimes Wolfe-Webber would feel constrained to flee from this compulsive hunger by escaping to crowded and enormous places like the Hofbrau Haus in Munich. There, sitting among strangers, he would feel himself caught up in "the warmth, the surge, the powerful communion of those enormous bodies, gulped down from stone mugs liter after liter of the cold and powerful dark beer . . . swung and roared and sang and shouted in the swaying mass. . . ." Being in visceral contact with the Volk made him feel alive and responsive in every pore. He did not yet recognize the destructive, murderous, fury that was potential in these prodigious displays of group élan.

At first, seduced by the adulation shown him, Wolfe was blind to the atmosphere of fear and repression in the country. In her book *Through Embassy Eyes* (pp. 90-91; Harcourt, Brace and World, Inc., 1939), Martha Dodd describes from firsthand observation the reception that Berliners gave him: "He became a legend around Berlin. . . . He seemed to give a sort of animation to the streets and cafés. . . . He gave back to the intellectual and creative people of Berlin a sense of their past, of their dignity and power and freedom of mind not under stress. Certainly he was the most vital experience literary Berlin had had in the Hitler years, and for months after, people would gather to talk of him." Then, gradually, he became aware of what was happening to a populace living under the heel of tyranny. He wrote in *You Can't Go Home Again* (p. 728; Harper & Brothers, 1940):

> I don't know why it was that people so unburdened themselves to me, a stranger, unless it was because they knew the love I bore them and their land. They seemed to feel a desperate need to talk to someone who would understand. . . . They told me stories of their friends and relatives who said unguarded things in public and disappeared without a trace, stories of the Gestapo, stories of neighbors' quarrels and petty personal spite turned into political persecution, stories of concentration

camps and pogroms, stories of rich Jews stripped and
beaten and robbed of everything they had and then denied the right to earn a pauper's wage, stories of well-
bred Jewesses despoiled and turned out of their homes
and forced to kneel and scrub off anti-Nazi slogans
scribbled on the sidewalks while young barbarians
dressed like soldiers formed a ring and prodded them
with bayonets and made the quiet places echo with the
shameless laughter of their mockery. It was a picture of
the Dark Ages come again—shocking beyond belief, but
true as the hell that man forever creates for himself.
. . . I recognized at last, in all its frightful aspects, the
spiritual disease which was poisoning unto death a noble
and a mighty people.

When Wolfe recognized this, it was time for him to leave the
country.

This, then, was the way I summed up Wolfe's involvement
with Germany. How did the students respond? They readily recognized his Faustian rage for quantitative experience, his com-
pelling need to celebrate "bigness" and "manyness." And they
understood, too, what was potentially dangerous in the atavistic
urge of his protagonists to sweep away the restraints of civilized
behavior. The trouble with his kind of élan, one of the students
said, is that it can lead to Hitlerism. Up to a certain point, he
added, energy and appetite are good. It is good to have romantic faith and enthusiasm. But Wolfe did not value proportion
and restraint enough. If a man does not know what his *limits*
are, he begins to think of himself as a superman. Then the trouble begins. Ordinary men, common pleasures, and satisfactions
are not enough for him. I am powerful, he keeps saying to himself, until he becomes convinced that a special destiny is looking
after him. Soon you hear him calling certain people *Untermenschen*. So look what has happened to our romantic naïf.
From a lover of life, he has become a destroyer. Thus romantic
excess can lead to blitzkrieg and, ultimately, to Auschwitz.

Another student remarked: "I see much of the German people through the writings of Thomas Wolfe. So many of us are romantics, dreamers. We truly want to be idealists. So far so good, yes? Then what goes wrong? From romantic innocents we become dangerous egotists. We act like the world is *only* the way we see it. No wonder that they begin to hate us, to call us the arrogant Germans." He added: "Hitler would have understood that Wolfe liked everything big. Big countries, big buildings, big appetites. The Führer, too, was in love with bigness—big autobahns, big rallies, big armies. Also, Hitler, too, thought of himself as an artist. He prided himself on being very sensitive. Oh, yes. . . . Isn't it a sad fact that sometimes a thin line separates the artist from the killer?"

These comments were representative of the students' overall response to the literary temperament of Wolfe. Altogether, the impression I have is that they recognized in him some qualities of their putative national traits, qualities that such informed thinkers as Thomas Mann and Jakob Wassermann, among others, have associated with the German character: romantic excess, an attachment to quantitative experience, a straining for metaphysical absolutes, an almost fanatical and certainly destructive attraction to vitalism for its own sake. At the least, they grasped the paradox that the agonies and exuberances of the romantic may impel him to pick up a pen and write soaring poetry or to turn the pages of Goethe with reverence; with that same hand, he may slay defenseless human beings.

The question of Wolfe and his Jewish characters came up for discussion. Most of the students had grown up without having befriended or, in some cases, without even having been acquainted with a single Jew, and they were curious to read what Wolfe had to say about them. At the outset, they were a little thrown by some of his grotesquely depicted Jewish characters. I explained that Wolfe's distorted treatment was not intended to be deliberately anti-Semitic; rather it was exercised in the same nagging key in which he complained about the provincials of his hometown, the precious aesthetes at Harvard, the dilettantes of the theatrical world. Actually, he was envious of the Jews that he observed, because they had the very qualities denied by his own temperament: laughter, ease, balance, moderation.

To point up Wolfe's essential attitude toward his Jewish characters, I focused on the much-praised portrayal of Frederick Jack in the posthumous novel, *You Can't Go Home Again*. What especially characterizes Jack, a successful businessman, is that he is very comfortable in his world. This relationship is in marked contrast to George Webber, a young Southern writer, who feels rootless and alienated in New York. The people he sees on the streets seem to him broken in spirit, and they exacerbate his feelings of transience.

Unlike Webber, Jack sees order and permanence everywhere he looks in the city. The tides of sidewalk humanity in all their protean movements are for him tonic. Further, he knows how to enjoy, and to stimulate others to enjoy, material things. He has an appreciative eye for elegant furnishings and well-made clothes. Indeed, it is Jack's graceful use of the creature comforts that leads Webber, who had been raised in a depressed boardinghouse atmosphere, to comment, extravagantly: "There is, of course, no greater fallacy than the one about the stinginess of Jews. They are the most lavish and opulent race on earth."

In Webber's eyes, Jack's most admirable trait is his sense of loyalty. He is generous to a fault, even to servants who had filched from him. He would go to great lengths to help a friend. Webber, whose home background had been filled with violent quarrels and enmity between family members, was impressed on attending one of Jack's parties because the Jews there seemed to him "together." (But if it is well that Webber was so cerebrally impressed, sitting there, beside these German students, I thought, not without bitterness, that Wolfe's protagonist never truly understood the terrible price Jews have paid over the centuries, enduring slavery, the Inquisition, the Crusades, closed medevial ghettos, pogroms, and genocide in order, yes, to remain "together.")

What Webber comes to recognize is that, in contrast to his

own self-destructive excesses, for Jack "ripeness is all." He had accepted the limits of his morality; he believed that wisdom lay in proportioning and focusing his ambitions and by effecting a proper relationship to his world. He consistently valued the middle way.

In sum, Webber respected Jack because he was generous, judicious, and loyal. And Wolfe seemed to be groping toward the key to the secret of Jack's sense of well-being in speculating that perhaps "some great inheritance of suffering, the long, dark ordeal of his race, had left him, as a precious distillation, this gift of balanced understanding." It is a gift that, clearly, the seminar students, looking at Jack through Wolfe's eyes, admired.

I did nothing to discourage such appreciation.

6

CHRISTMAS AND BROTHERHOOD

"SCHNEE! SCHNEE! [snow]," Frau Baier was crying as we awoke one mid-December morning. She was on the front sidewalk before the house, energetically shoveling snow, several inches of which had fallen in the night. A few flakes were still descending. The first snow of the year and the first my California-bred children had ever seen. Danny was alarmed. "She'll shovel it all up. There won't be any snow left," he said. Tam assured him that Frau Baier would leave enough. Dina was all for going outdoors at once and catching snowflakes on her tongue. Jon was unhappy because he had a case of enlarged tonsils that would keep him indoors.

Looking up at us, Frau Baier waved her arms gleefully. "Come out!" she cried, and swooping up snow, she flung it like confetti over her head.

So we bundled Dina and Danny into warm hooded jackets, and they left the house. Standing at the window, Tam and I saw how at first Danny shivered, his face and hands stung by the cold, and how Dina kept her head down, as though fearing that the snow, this sudden world of whiteness, might be dangerous quicksand. But Frau Baier, bless her, got them into the spirit of the moment. She bent and made some snowballs. Soon she and the kids were wildly tossing snow in one another's faces.

Later Frau Baier gave the kids a sled ride. In her zeal to introduce them to this sport, she was running. Dina and Danny chortled with immense pleasure. "Hitler should have seen this," I said to Tam. "An honest German frau—one of the 'eternal mothers of the nation,' as the Führer used to refer to German women—pulling Jewish children over the snow!"

The day before Christmas. Ice on the ground, snow on the gabled roofs, and that morning Tam and I came downstairs from the third floor to find Frau Baier in the first-floor living room, working over a Christmas tree. "This is for you," she said, grinning. The shutters were down, the lights out, and twelve white candles, resting on the branches, burned. A paper, gold-winged angel decorated the top of the tree and at its base was a cardboard stable. Inside it were the adoring parents; they stood to one side of the crib containing the infant Jesus. Before the manger were a large dish of Bavarian candy and four or five oranges.

The tree was a complete surprise. She had put it up while we were still asleep. Now the good woman was smiling like a kid who has been up to mischief.

"*Schön?*" she asked. "Beautiful, beautiful," Tam assured her. "My father is turning over in his grave," she whispered to me. "Very nice," I said dryly, wondering how she reconciled this tree with her awareness that we were Jews.

Encouraged by our compliments, Frau Baier brought forth packages of long-stemmed sparklers and lighted them. Then she went upstairs and quickly returned with Sigi and set him to playing on the accordion "Silent Night!" and "O Little Town of Bethlehem."

We had come to Germany, to Nuremberg, to Julius Streicher territory, to have our first Christmas tree. Well, what purpose would it have served had I, in that moment, reminded her that Germans weren't very Christmasy in their treatment of Jews during the Hitler years? Yes, and when synagogues were set afire, was that a sign of peace and goodwill to *all* men?

She brought us a gargantuan plate of sponge cake and a pot of coffee. Sigi continued to swing out on the accordion. With enthusiasm, with fervor, our kids lighted more candles for the tree. All was *gemütlich.*

Still, it seemed to me that the gold-winged angel was looking down at the scene below with cool detachment, perhaps even boredom. And despite our noisy festivity, Jesus hadn't stirred in his cradle. He hadn't yet been dragged to Calvary, nailed on the cross; and in his name, century after century, Jews terrorized and destroyed. . . .

Did the angel know that less than two miles from this room Hitler had once mounted a platform and exhorted his beloved Nuremberg populace to be pitilessly hard on international Jewry?

That a few miles from this room stores owned by Jews were smashed on Crystal Night?

Now, twenty years later, before the tree, Frau Baier had her arms affectionately around Tam's shoulders. The kids, squealing with pleasure, blew out the candles.

Tam and I had often wondered where Sigi went with his sled after school. Frau Baier would casually refer to the name of the place. Then one afternoon in late January, Sigi brought the kids and me there.

We came to a forest preserve with high hills, trails, towering trees, scores of sledders, many dressed in Bavarian green hose, boots, and Alpine hats. Altogether, it was a festive white-winter carnival scene that Bruegel would have painted with delight.

Presently, among those carrying sleds to the top of a long, steep slope, red-coated and hooded, went Dina, Dan, and Jon, led by Sigi.

Middle-aged, brittle-boned, and sensible, I stayed below.

It was a good ten minutes' climb to the top of the run. After a while I could no longer see them; perhaps they had disappeared around a bend.

But other sledders were visible, and they came careening, streaking, and skidding down the slope. Sometimes a sled overturned, spilling its rider. Elderly men and women stood on the rear of sleds, children seated in front of them, and coolly steered a course between the Scylla and Charybdis of trees and rocks, taking the precipitous run as though it were a cakewalk. Squat and thick-legged middle-aged women calmly balanced on the sleds as confidently as rodeo cowboys astride steers. And then some local children, dumply-faced, pig-tailed, and leder-hosened, came hurtling down the run.

Now it was the turn of the first of the Halperin kids, Danny, with Sigi sitting behind him. They expertly navigated a hairpin curve, swerved sharply around a tree and made a long smooth descent to the street below—unaccompanied by shuddering Götterdämmerung music.

Then Sigi took Dina down. Then Jon. Each time my heart blanched, fear pulled in my stomach. I worried that they might crash into a tree. But there were no spills, no accidents. Their red coats and hoods flamed through the descending trees. They came through each run smiling, their cheeks blooming in the clear-blue frosty air. With each descent they stood taller. On to Garmisch! On to the Matterhorn!

A couple hours later, with sniffling noses and frosted cheeks, numbed fingers and toes, we were homeward bound. The kids sat on the sled while, reindeer-yoked, their father pulled them over the icy streets, singing: "Yo ho, yo ho, it's off to work we go. . . ." Sigi practiced the one Americanism he knew best: "It was okay?" *"Prima! Prima!"* Dina responded gleefully. Sigi said that for the next time he knew of an even higher hill and faster run. Danny broke out, "Let's go *now!*"

7

THE DARK FACE

CHRISTMAS TREES, accordion music and brotherly love, snow and sledding do not a Hitler make. Where was the other face of Germany, the murderous one that might explain the criminal acts of 1933–1945? Where was it hiding? One January night I saw what may have been an intimation of this face.

While on an after-dinner walk, I went along a road so dark and devoid of houses that one saw the matchlights held by oncoming people long before their bodies or faces became visible. Here and there small vegetable gardens bordered the sides of the road. About a mile away from the Baier home, I passed what once had been a castle and now was a residence for retired railroad workers. Infrequently, a car came by, sometimes a solitary walker. The tall trees along the way were dwarfed under a darkly impenetrable sky.

I should not have noticed that the place was a *Gasthaus* if not for the beer sign nailed to the top of a small wooden stairway just off the road. The latter led down some steps to what appeared to be simply another of the wooden garden shacks that are indigenous to that area. Except this shack had lights burning dimly behind its clapboard shutters. There was a faded sign over its doorway advertising the name of a *Gasthaus*. Did the sign apply to the present, I wondered, or did it stand from some bygone day? Could there actually be a *Gasthaus* in this isolated place?

I went down the steps. Directly beyond the last one was a muddy dirt courtyard, in a corner of which was a primitive outdoor latrine. Standing in the courtyard, I faintly heard the sound of music and singing coming from behind the shutters. A few yards before me was not, as I had first thought, a garden shack but rather a one-story dwelling.

A moment later I had left the twentieth century and entered the world of Hieronymus Bosch. Afterward, I would say to Tam that the other Germany was here, the one with the dark face.

An old-fashioned wood-burning stove and a large round wooden table dominated the center of an otherwise threadbare room. Close to this center table were several smaller rectangular ones. Elbow to elbow, flesh to flesh—an arrangement, which, I sensed, they required—sat the customers. A jukebox was pounding out raucous Bavarian drinking songs. On the walls a sign, POLICE FORBIDDEN, and also a poster depicting a bleary-eyed solitary drinker lifting a beer mug to his lips, and the legend underneath read: "Don't mourn the good old days when there is drink before you."

The customers, a gristly-looking lot, were drinking, playing cards, devouring sausages and heavy bread, stretching their hulking bodies and leathery necks. I sensed that they had been there for some time. It was warm and communal here, perhaps more so than where they lived. Their bodies were in close physical proximity, skin beside skin; they drew heat from one another in this ancestral cave. The great blood brotherhood of the Volk?

There they were, slamming cards down on the tables, shouting drunkenly into one another's faces, laughing coarsely when two men squirted fluid from water pistols into each other's eyes. These were the muscle boys who, universally, like noise, drink, and brawls.

Gradually, I recognized those faces from my early Chicago days when I worked on unskilled labor jobs in shops and factories. I remembered how some of those workers had expelled gas for laughs and spoken about lovemaking as though it were syn-

onymous with human excrement. How they had stuffed their
mouths with heavy sausage meats and limned every other sen-
tence with Abie and jewed down and kike.

And here in the *Gasthaus* were these same bestial faces. Put
guns in the hands of some of the Chicago types I have referred
to, and they would have shot victims as routinely as the most
dedicated SS personnel. The difference is that among those in
this room there had to be some who had once raised their arms
to the Führer. It is even possible that one of them had held a
gun that had toppled Jews into open graves.

There was a custom they practiced which, to my uninitiated
eyes, was terrifying. On entering, a customer went slowly and
heavily around the room and knocked once on each tabletop.
Same ritual on leaving. One knock only, a loud, blunt rap. An
old Nuremberg custom dating back to the Middle Ages, one of
my students later explained. What did the knock signify to those
sitting at the tables? That you were friend not enemy, that you
had not come to pillage, to burn down or rape, but rather to
drink together. Hence the identifying rap on the table, like a secret password, and then the newcomer sat down beside peasant
faces that might have been painted by Bosch. Even now I hear
that sound, recalling for me the peremptory knock of the SS on
the doors of flats in European ghettos; the knock which signified
that the SS had arrived to take Jews to the *Umschlagplatz*. . . .

What should I have done—gone from table to table, knock-
ing on each, asking: "Do you hate Jews? Did you hate them
when Hitler was chief?" Take it easy, I said to myself. You're
not in any danger. They don't have to suspect that you're a Jew.
Let them assume that you're just another curious American.
And they probably had adduced that I was an American from
the cut of my jacket and slacks, the style of my shoes.

Sitting there, I sensed that behind the veneer of Volk frater-
nity, behind the beer-swilling and sausage-fressing, the rough-
house conversation and the tribal dependency of flesh upon
flesh, was the brute presence of a potentially murderous force, a
force that someday could once again surge with the compulsion

to kill, kill . . . And once more the windows of Jewish homes would be smashed or their buildings bombed, and in the end Jews would disappear into night and fog. So much hate and violence behind those outwardly *gemütlich* faces. In a *Gasthaus* where people sit close, rap on tables, raise stone mugs in unison and move them menacingly in one another's faces, stamp on the floors, whistle, lock arms, and sing in thickly raucous voices—in such a place they once could well have thundered *Deutschland über alles*. And perhaps they still yearn for The Leader. Or, at the least, for another Crystal Night. Perhaps they remember the Nazi days with fondness because Hitler gave them free vacations, built the autobahns, kept the streets clear of crime and corrupt foreigners. Perhaps some still dream that the beloved Führer is alive somewhere.

What macabre hoax was History playing here! It was like looking through the viewer of a diorama. First a scene showing Jews being struck and driven through the streets of Nuremberg. Then, in the next scene, a *Gasthaus* set down amid darkness and garden plots, and patrons with Hieronymus Bosch faces. Then perhaps for the most bizarre touch of all, the image of an American Jew safely sitting among the others, in a place where twenty years before he might well have paid for such patronage with his life.

I rose, left the *Gasthaus,* and went back uneasily along the dark road to the house that the Baiers had built in Hitler's favorite Nuremberg.

8

TWO MORAL HEROES

LOOKING BACK, I can recognize that the second phase of our stay in Germany began with our initial attendance in mid-November 'at the meeting of the Amerika Haus discussion group. Then, in late February, the invitation for the talk at Frankfurt arrived, marking the start of the third phase.

There was a phone call from the young German attached to the American Embassy in Bonn. He was calling to inquire whether I would be interested in speaking in Frankfurt on the occasion of Brotherhood Week in mid-March. It seemed that a Frankfurter Society for Christian-Jewish Cooperation—to that point I had never heard of this group, which apparently has a membership in a number of West German cities—was looking for a speaker. The organization had contacted him, and he thought, remembering our previous conversations aboard the *Queen Mary,* that I might be interested. He indicated that the nature of the topic would be left to my own discretion.

I said that I would like to think about the possibility and call him back in a day or two. My first impulse was to decline the invitation. To prepare a talk would mean days away from some writing I was doing at the time. Then, too, I wondered what was expected of me. Did they, the official at the Embassy and the Society membership, expect me to deliver a "pro-German" talk? If so, then I would be better advised to eschew any public statements that went beyond what was normally involved in lectures at the university.

Then I remembered that the trial of the former Auschwitz guards was going on in Frankfurt, and the thought occurred to me that a speech in this "sensitive" locale might do its bit toward keeping a hard light focused on the recent past.

On the second day following his call, I phoned the Bonn official and accepted the invitation, indicating that I proposed to speak on the observations of an American-Jewish professor in postwar Germany. It may be that the talk will be critical of certain aspects of the postwar German scene, I forewarned him. That's quite all right, he said readily. Yes, but does he *really* mean that? I wondered.

Thus did I attempt to trammel my misgivings about accepting the invitation. Misgivings? No, that is hardly precise enough. I must have been more than a little eager to accept the invitation. Because, to begin with, knowing nothing about the Society, I might have queried the Bonn official, asked him whether it was possible to get some literature on the history, activities, and objectives of this organization. Or I might have inquired about the linkup, if any, between the American Embassy and the Society. Why, after all, would the Embassy be interested in sponsoring this group? And why the United States-owned Amerika Haus as the place for the talk? Yet, despite these unanswered questions, I had accepted the invitation.

I set to work on the speech. The time was late February, and the talk was scheduled for March 11. The days and nights in Nuremberg were fiercely cold—at least they were so for a Californian. Seated at my desk, I sometimes wore two pairs of socks, a field jacket, and a woolen scarf. But the deeper freeze was on the paper. From the beginning, the writing went badly. The facts, quotations, raw material I had assembled, but lacking was a point of view, a perspective. All too plainly, I did not know what I really thought about the German youth we had met or about the complicated question of German-Jewish reconciliation or, more importantly, about the appropriate stance of a visiting American-Jewish academic.

A week went by without much writing to show for my sitting at a desk for several hours a day. Finally, I went to see Rabbi

David Shapiro, hoping he would say something that would help to unfreeze the block. Rabbi Shapiro is the religious leader of a Jewish community in Fürth. Originally from Warsaw, he is of Rabbinic and Hasidic stock; his father-in-law was the eldest of the Warsaw rabbis. In the final days of the Warsaw ghetto, Rabbi Shapiro and two other rabbis, the last three rabbis remaining in the ghetto, were offered an opportunity by the Court of the Bishops in Warsaw to escape to a safe hiding place in another part of the city. They were asked to deliberate on this unusual offer and make their decision at once, for the total destruction of Warsaw Jewry seemed imminent.

The three rabbis withdrew to discuss the matter but instead fell into a deep silence. Each wanted to live for himself and for the sake of his family. Rabbi Shapiro had a wife and four children—and yet he wanted to be true to his responsibility as a spiritual leader for the remaining Jews in the ghetto.

Finally, Rabbi Shapiro, the youngest of the three, broke the silence, and he said, as is reported by K. Shabbetai in "As Sheep to Slaughter":

> I am the youngest present. My words do not bind you.
> We all of us know perfectly well that one cannot help
> these folk in any way whatsoever. Yet by the very fact
> that we stay with them, that we do not forsake them,
> there is a kind of encouragement, something maybe of
> the only possible encouragement. I do not have the
> strength to abandon these people. (*World Jewry,* March-
> April, 1963).

He had spoken for the others. And so their only reply to the offer was a terse, "There cannot be any negotiation about this matter."

Miraculously, Rabbi Shapiro survived (not so his wife and children) the destruction of the ghetto, was arrested by the Germans, and sent from one concentration camp to another, five in all. In the winter of 1944-1945, he and other prisoners were forced to march nearly two hundred kilometers from a camp near Nuremberg to Dachau. His feet and legs were badly frozen and became abnormally large, and he was barely alive when they reached Dachau.

Advancing Allied troops liberated the camp; his own brother, Abraham, then a Jewish chaplain in the U.S. Army and now a professor of Jewish studies on an American campus, was among the liberators. Until the moment of their reunion in a charnel house, the brothers had had no contact for years. What words can describe that moment when the two embraced each other? Abraham Shapiro took his brother away from Dachau and brought him to Fürth, the seat of an ancient Jewish community, because there was a need for him here. A small community of some one hundred and thirty observant Jews, many of them displaced persons from Poland, gratefully took him as their rabbi. Since then, on the strength of his reputation as a Talmudic scholar, he has been offered rabbinical posts in other European cities, but he prefers to stay in Fürth, guiding his small congregation.

I sat beside him in his study. Full and entirely gray, his beard has an elegantly patriarchal cast. He is in his sixties. His eyes are tremendously alert, and he moves with force and decisiveness. Over his short sturdy figure he wears a black caftanlike robe.

The study is on the second floor of an old tenementlike building hidden away in a bleak street of Fürth. Since the city's main synagogue was destroyed by the SS in 1939, the spiritual needs of the present congregation are served by a small synagogue in the tenementlike building, whose residents are almost entirely composed of the Rabbi's following.

We conversed in Yiddish, the language almost exclusively spoken in my grandfather's flat in Chicago during the '20s and '30s.

I told him about what I had been hearing from some young Germans in Nuremberg. "Rabbi, what shall I say to these young people?" I asked. His reply was immediate, blunt. "Tell them the truth. Tell them—boys, your fathers murdered my fathers.

And this we will not—must not—forget!" He paused, reflected. "Yes, tear away the scales from their eyes."

In my lifetime I have heard hundreds of people use the word "murdered." But when this man uttered the words "your fathers murdered my fathers," they slashed through my consciousness like a knife.

Yet there wasn't hate in his voice or face but rather only the passionate conviction of a man who has suffered, who has earned the right to be absolutely blunt.

I related that some of my students at the university had spoken to me about their sense of horror and shame over the destruction of European Jewry.

"I know what they say with their mouths," he said quickly, pointing to his lips. "But what do they feel here?" He touched his breast.

"Rabbi, some Jews I know say we must hate the Germans for what happened—that we must never forgive them." And here I cited a passage from an article, "An Assignment with Hate," by one of the most important writers and prophets of our time, Elie Wiesel:

> I cry out with all my heart against forgiveness, against forgetting, against silence. Every Jew, somewhere in his being, should set apart a zone of hate—healthy, virile hate—for what the German personifies and for what persists in the German. To do otherwise would be a betrayal of the dead. (*Commentary*, December, 1962, p. 476.)

He shook his head. "The Torah bids us to remember Amalek, not to hate it." And then he added, citing the words of Ezekiel: "The son shall not suffer for the iniquity of the father." A moment later, as though in an afterthought, he broke out, "We must lift up *Menschen*. Lift up."

When he speaks you believe him. When he says "lift up," you can imagine him going from barracks to barracks in the camps, buoying up the spirits of others. And with what fire did he speak! An immense power burns in his eyes and voice. No wonder they were unable to kill him! I thought. Even the SS must have felt the indestructibleness of the man.

"Rabbi, some people say that the Jews in the camps should have risen against the guards, that they should have gone to their deaths fighting back."

"How do you fight back against such a monster when you are without weapons? Even so, when Jews went with upraised heads to the gas chambers, singing *Ani Maamin,* 'I Believe,' this was like a lead pipe against the Nazis. It was the same as striking them. This is how a Jew should die—with his head high, back straight. The Torah tells us how during the reign of Nebuchadnezzar, Jews leaped into the fire, wearing their finest clothes as a sign of contempt for their murderers and because they were dying with perfect faith in God. Faith—this is important. In the camps some would ask, 'Rabbi, do you really believe that one day we shall walk out beyond that barbed wire?' 'Yes,' I said, 'I believe it.'

" 'I believe it!' " he repeated, his face flaming. "And it has come to pass. Later I met one who had been with me in Dachau and he said, 'Rabbi, you were right!' " He paused, and his voice seemed to search, to reach far back into the darkness of the past. "I saw some of them who did not believe," he said quietly, slowly. "They fell away," he gestured, as though describing a falling movement.

Again he paused, and his eyes took on a distant look. "On the days of hard labor, there would be blackness in their faces. I see them. . . ." He paused, shook his head slightly. "Then someone would tell them to sing and suddenly they would be singing with all their hearts. For a little while they would forget their troubles."

He was smiling, faintly, as though he were trying to convey something without words. My God, I thought, he has come out of such a hell, has lost a wife and four children, and can still smile! And I wondered—is *that* what I should say at Frankfurt? To lift up their heads and be *worthy* of their spiritual distress?

If the Jewish people could rise up out of the charnel houses, it should be no less possible for them to carry their burden of collective shame with *consent* and with dignity.

As I was leaving, the Rabbi said, referring to the coming Frankfurt talk, "Let what passes from your lips come from your heart."

Going through the streets of Fürth, I heard his voice—"Lift up!" And on returning home, I said to my wife, "Well, now I have seen what faith is."

A few days later I spoke with another moral hero of our time, Probst Heinrich Grueber, of the Evangelical Church in Berlin. He is well known for his courageous opposition to the Nazis and his help to European Jews. His defiance of the Third Reich landed him in Dachau, where he was nearly murdered. After the war he helped establish an old-age residence in Berlin-Dahlem for victims of the Nuremberg Laws. He was the only German to testify against Eichmann at the Jerusalem trial. And for many years he has been active in promoting the exchange of visits between the youth of Israel and Germany.

He had come to Nuremberg for a day to speak on a program in connection with Brotherhood Week. I phoned his hotel, and he agreed to a meeting.

We conversed in English. His speech has a sharpness, a thrust—the incisiveness of a man who has attained a compression in his own life. Altogether, he gives the impression of being a man who meets existence with the utmost directness. His eyes are steady and bright, and they look squarely at you. His mouth and jaw suggest a rock-ribbed stubborn honesty.

At the outset, leaning forward, he warned that it might be difficult for me to hear him because his teeth were knocked out by an SS man at Dachau, and since then the clarity of his speech has been impaired. He hastened to add that his sufferings were as nothing compared to what Jews in the camps experienced.

After I summarized what I had been hearing from members

of the Amerika Haus discussion group and from my students at
the university, he nodded and said: "I always say two things
when I talk to the younger generation here. First, it is their
moral responsibility to assume the burdens for the crimes of
their elders—and they must not carry them grudgingly."

"Burdens *willingly* assumed?" I interjected.

"Yes," he agreed. "Yes, that's it . . . and second, I tell them
that it is their responsibility to act in their everyday lives to help
prevent the rise of another Hitler. I see now that if one hundred
clergymen, in the early days of the Third Reich, had protested
against Hitler, things might have been different. I cannot say I
did my best, and I know nobody who can say that of himself."

"Well, you went to a concentration camp because you were
opposed to him on principle."

"No," he said quietly, shaking his head, "by then it was too
late. That is why we must be alert now. Most of us hasten to
defer to majority opinions when it is not always necessary to do
so. Men should know when to say no. There ought to be a line
beyond which they will not compromise."

As he spoke, I found myself thinking: Well, this is, after all,
an exceptional man, a hero. How many people would risk their
lives and the safety of their families? So then I asked him how
he felt during the time he was openly opposing the Third Reich,
knowing full well that his actions placed his wife and three children in extreme danger.

He answered without delay. "When God puts a man on the
road it is not for him to get off it for his family's sake. They
must expect to take risks along with him. I myself never seriously considered that I should stop speaking up because of what
might happen to my family. I know I could be killed or sent to
the camps, but I said Thy will be done, even if it means my
death."

Then I said that some Jews believe it is important for every
Jew to set aside a zone of hate in his heart for all Germans, and
I quoted the passage from Elie Wiesel's "An Assignment with
Hate."

The Dean replied that he did not believe in the necessity of hate. When the SS man at Dachau knocked out his teeth, he had prayed for him. "In Jerusalem I said to Eichmann: 'You sent me to Dachau and you were hard on my family but I don't hate you.'" He leaned forward and said, carefully, "Hate begets hate and hate must be done away with." A familiar enough cliché, of course, but coming from a man like Grueber, it was one of those clichés which staggers the listener with the weight of its force.

He recalled that when he was in Israel on a recent visit, President Zalman Shazar said to him: "I want to thank you for three things. First, for the friend you have been to the Jewish people. Second, for giving testimony at the Eichmann trial. But more importantly, for saying what you did about the need to do away with hate. Ever since you made the statement many young Israelis, who heretofore did not want to accept the hand of friendship extended to them by Germans, have had a change of heart."

As our meeting came to a close, the Dean wished me luck at Frankfurt and added that though it was important for the younger generation to atone for the crimes of their fathers, it was equally important for Jews from abroad like myself "to talk to the young people here and check whether they are on the right road."

Well, it was reassuring to hear that he thought I was on the "right road" in Germany, because, frankly, the professor himself was not so certain of his direction.

9

SPEAKING OUT
IN FRANKFURT AND ELSEWHERE

FRANKFURT. Where in the late eighteenth century, Jews were locked up at night, like cattle, in a wretched ghetto. Where once Jews were ordered to lower their voices, to avoid offending Christian ears.

I was on the platform before some one hundred and fifty people. Their faces looked intent, sober, watchful. They seemed to be in their twenties and thirties, though I spotted a few middle-aged and elderly people. Tam sat in one of the back rows. A copy of the address, "An American-Jewish Professor in Postwar Germany," was before me on the lectern.

Even in that moment it occurred to me that my self-appointed role as a public Jew in Germany was absurd. Who was I, a sheltered American, to represent the millions who had been destroyed? Be careful there, my best friend had admonished before we left for Germany. "Don't be seduced, don't let them use you to speak in behalf of instant redemption." I have his exact words in a letter, his response to my acceptance of the invitation to speak in Frankfurt.

> What I find most difficult is that you should want to
> stand up before audiences, testifying to your Jewish
> identity, when that same admission made in your youth
> would have cost your life and the lives of your family.
> So the only one, to my mind, who now has the right to

make that admission is not one who has gone scot free, who did not have inhuman things done to him, but someone who paid the price and knows the cost. Let him, not you, speak on this problem of German youth.

But would what my friend advocated really have been better? *Who* would have been better for it? The German people did not speak up when Hitler raged. *You must not be silent*— isn't that what the Holocaust dead and survivors enjoin us, the living, who will to be free men?

Anyway, the fact is that I did speak in Frankfurt, whether unwisely or well. And now I should like to reproduce that talk along with some retrospective comments on it. Why the commentary on the text? Perhaps this is a way of belatedly "squaring the record," of coming "clean." It is perhaps a second chance for dealing with some lingering qualms over having given that talk in Frankfurt and elsewhere.

"Some of my students and acquaintances here are sensitive to the dark history of the Third Reich," I began. "They believe that not only their parents' generation stands accused but themselves as well, and they resent feeling that they are on trial for crimes they themselves did not commit. As one of my students put it: 'We feel that history has placed us on a cross.' Often they are tempted to detach themselves from that cross, to walk away from it—and yet they do not feel free to do so. 'It's a burden we cannot shake off,' they say. They see themselves as doomed to keep serving penance for the crimes of their fathers."

[There is no denying that these young people are well-intentioned and concerned. But the semblance of self-pity in their eyes and voices when we spoke together, this is what I should have stressed early in the talk and not merely glossed over.]

"So it is that some have made pilgrimages of penance to Dachau and Bergen-Belsen, and others have gone to Israel to work there for a time. The sister of one student is living in a kibbutz.

In the beginning, members of the settlement did not know that she is a German, for she spoke a flawless English. When finally her national identity became known, given its strict policy against admitting German repentants, the community held a special meeting. So unanimously was she liked by the kibbutz membership that it encouraged her to stay on. Daily now, in one of those strange historical juxtapositions, she works beside those who wear on their flesh the tattooed numbers of the Nazi concentration camps.

"Perhaps these students have earned the right to resent their burden of collective shame, earned it through ordeals of terror and hardship during the war and early postwar years. Their lives were hardly featherbedded. Some have informed me, without the intent to elicit sympathy, how during the late '40s they often sat in dim, unheated classrooms. They were not unfamiliar with hunger. They felt paralyzed, old. So I believe that their hard years have given them the right to speak up.

"Quite often they remind me of the young Americans I knew in the '30s. We too were troubled, restive, disgruntled; we were impatient with the perspectives and actions of the older generation. Yet I have been given to understand, both from what has been written on the subject and from what I have heard from knowledgeable Germans, that this is not an accurate analogy, and that the two generations ought not to be compared. These sources maintain that students in today's Germany tend to eschew patriotic nationalism and to reject politics as a means of ameliorating their country's spiritual distress. According to some German educators, they are more conservative, skeptical, and undramatic than were the young Americans of the '30s I knew. Perhaps so. Then perhaps what I mean to suggest is that the temper of the students here often strikes one as quite similar to that of the young American Jews I knew in the '30s. So that when one of my students recently told me that he has encountered anti-German sentiments from European students, I heard the echo of other voices from another time in the United States. 'You go to a dance at a European university,' he said, 'and the students are friendly—until they find out you are a German. And then they deliberately freeze you out of their company. Or sometimes they begin attacking you for what happened in concentration camps. They keep after you, won't let you forget the past. It will take years before they stop accusing us,' he concluded glumly. Then I think to myself: supposing he is overly prone to feeling slighted, does that make his state of mind any less real? For the fact is he believes he is discriminated against because he is German, just as in the '30s many of us supposed —more often than not with good reason—that when we applied for certain positions or sought admission into certain professional and social organizations, we were discriminated against because we were Jews.

"Given this corner of my past, perhaps this is why I am inclined to listen carefully when students here say to me, urgently, as though in a cry of hopeless protest against any silent accusations I might be harboring against them, 'Try to understand.' *Try to understand.* Even now I can hear them saying to me: 'We realize that what happened here was inexcusable. But try to understand how it could have happened. How step by step the population could have been intimidated, silenced. We'll give you our interpretation. We won't try to pretty up the facts. We won't try to explain away the quiescence of our elders which made Dachau possible. But if you, as is the case with many foreign visitors, don't really want an exchange of thought, if you insist upon interrogating and accusing us, then please go your own way. Please leave us alone. We just can't go on endlessly feeling guilty, apologetic. And, incidentally, it doesn't make us happy to observe that many tourists from abroad, on first coming to Nuremberg, rush out with cameras to Zeppelin Wiese, simply because Hitler held his annual party demonstrations there. Mouths agape, they stare up at the place in the stands from which he made his speeches. They look around, as though picturing the marchers, torches, banners. Sometimes you get the feeling that they are looking at the place through eyes which have seen too many Cecil B. De Mille extravaganzas. Zeppelin

Wiese is not all of Nuremberg. And, frankly, it amuses and sad-
dens us to see foreign science fiction books portraying diaboli-
cally evil Germans. Or detective books and cheap popular novels showing Germans as moustached, heel-clicking villains. This
is *not* us. Won't they see us as we really are?'

"Well, these have been some of my initial impressions. Many
young people want me to understand. Well and good. But understanding is a two-way street. Let *them* try to understand,
also. Let them grasp why it is so difficult for Jews to understand
or to refrain from judging. Let them understand why some do
not even want to understand but rather to hate. A hate that is
more than justified but necessary, because Jews have never sufficiently learned how to hate. Elie Wiesel, himself a concentration camp survivor, has one of his characters in *Dawn* (Hill &
Wang, Inc., 1962) say of the Jewish people:

> "Their tragedy, throughout the centuries, has stemmed
> from their inability to hate those who have humiliated
> and from time to time exterminated them. Now our only
> chances lies in . . . learning the necessity and art of
> hate. Otherwise . . . our future will only be an ex-
> tension of the past. . . .

"And in a *Commentary* article 'Appointment with Hate' (De-
cember, 1962), he presses the point:

> "There is a time to love and a time to hate; whoever
> does not hate when he should, does not desire to love
> when he is able. Perhaps, had we learned to hate more
> during the war years of ordeal, fate itself would have
> taken fright. The Germans did their best to teach us,
> but we were poor pupils in the discipline of hate. . . ."

[I remember our meeting with Elie Wiesel, this great
prophetic writer, in New York the night before we sailed for
Germany. He came to our hotel room in Manhattan. His eyes!
They will look at me for a lifetime. No wonder André Mauriac
wept at what he saw in them. They are haunted. He has come

back from the grave, from the realm of the dead. He has known immense suffering, and yet, astonishingly, not by a single word or gesture does the man appeal for pity. I could not meet his eyes. Before their steady gaze I cringed, seeing my impure innocence. . . . And yet to hate one's oppressors is sometimes easier said than done, as Wiesel himself discovered. He drastically cut short a visit to Germany in 1962; altogether, he was in the country for only forty-eight hours. He had felt impelled to flee it after finding himself unable to hate the Germans he met. In the same article he describes what happened to him:

> But finally, if I was compelled to cut short my visit and take the plane back to Paris after forty-eight hours, it was probably because I fell into the trap: I answered questions, I shook hands, I even smiled back. And then I could bear no more of this civilized behavior: I began to hate myself, having lost my taste for hating others.

[But what about me? Having chosen to stand before the lectern in Frankfurt, perhaps I, too, had fallen into a "trap," one of my own making.]

"I have said that understanding is a two-way street. Specifically, some of the young people I have met here need to realize that the anti-German sentiment they have experienced is insignificant compared to the centuries of persecution Jews have known. None of these young people was ever locked up behind ghetto walls. None of them was ever forced to wear the humiliating yellow badge. Granted, they knew hard times during the war. But in any accurate computation, would they even begin to compare their previous hardships with what concentration camp prisoners suffered? Or with the agonies of those non-Jewish Greeks who were systematically starved? Or with what the Russian populace suffered during the German Occupation?

"Moreover, how can they compare their burden with the kind that Jews in the modern world carry? Sartre has recognized the nature of this condition: 'I who am not a Jew, I have nothing to prove . . . but to be a Jew is to be thrown into—to be abandoned to—the situation of a Jew; and at the same time it is to be responsible in and through one's own person for the destiny and very nature of the Jewish people.' Would these young people fully understand—not merely as an intellectual abstraction but on their very pulses—what Sartre says about the difficulties of *choosing* oneself as a Jew? Would they understand what is behind the assertion made by Albert Memmi, in his brilliant study, *Portrait of a Jew*: 'To be a Jew is, naturally, not to have received as an out and out gift those traditional blessings of good fairies: a native land, nationality, a place in history, etc. . . . As a Jew, those things will be bitterly disputed us, granted, taken back again, questioned, so that rarely can we measure up naturally to the current social dimensions of most men'? And would they understand, from their depths, how two thousand years of grief is behind Ernie Levy's cry in *The Last of the Just,* 'To be a Jew is impossible'? Yet they resent the burden which the history of *merely* the last eighteen years has imposed upon them.

"At any rate, being sorry is not enough. Having an awakened conscience is not enough. The younger generation here must see to it that another Hitler does not emerge again. But enlightened vigilance depends upon knowledge. So I am wondering what German students are learning about Jewish history. What are they learning about the so-called duality of allegiance from which generation after generation of German Jews suffered? Can they, for example, trace Jewish history in Germany from the eighteenth century to the Nuremberg Racial Laws in 1935, when the slogan German and Jew was replaced by the iron command German *or* Jew? For it seems to me that such study would be all to the good."

[To this point in the talk the audience appeared to be listening closely. They certainly looked grave enough. I glanced in Tam's direction once or twice but her face, the little I could see of it in between the massed figures of the audience, revealed no clear indication of how she thought the speech was going.

[Then I turned to another matter—the question of judging

today's Germans because of the atrocities committed during the Hitler era.]

"First of all I find absurd the notion that an American Jew, who was comparatively safe during the war years, should come to Germany to judge Germans. Nor do I accept the suggestion that I should hate en masse the people here because of what happened during the Third Reich. Hate I do feel but it is directed against what took place during the twelve years of terror —the silencing of voices, the denial of human freedom. Hate I have for the accursed memory of Eichmann, who once proclaimed that he 'would leap laughing into his grave because the feeling that he had five million people on his conscience would be for him a source of extraordinary satisfaction.' Hate I have for the death of God in children, who within the long night of Auschwitz suddenly discovered absolute evil. Hate I have for the tragic disfiguration of guilt in the survivors of the camps."

[Truly hate? How much of the anger and outrage I profess to express over Eichmann, the atrocities, is deep-seated? For the self-conscious desire to feel even a portion of the anguish suffered by the survivors cannot alter the fact that I was *not* there, that what happened to European Jewry did *not* directly affect me and still seems distant to me. Even my attempts to pronounce such names as Bergen-Belsen, Maidenek, Janow, Skarzysko are strained.]

"But the much more important issue is the burden of our Jewish heritage. Informed Jews will generally agree that this burden has had negative as well as positive effects on the shaping of the Jewish people. It has blessed them with the capacity to endure suffering, extraordinary resilience, and a heightened will to live; they have a sturdy respect for family life and for the sanctity of human life itself. However, when seen by an individual Jew as oppressive and degrading, this burden has too often led to feelings of shame and self-hatred, with their consequent crippling effects on human character. In *Portrait of a Jew*, Memmi has described the Jew who has such negative feelings as the perfect example of a 'defendant.'

"He thinks and acts like a defendant: he is convinced that he is accused and conducts his life accord-
ingly. Looked upon as different, he considers himself
different. That is one of the most pertinent comments on
what might be called a philosophy of points of view: a
sustained point of view ends by becoming his very flesh."

[It pains me to realize that I said this. Why did I bring up
Memmi's controversial notions on the psychology of individual
Jews? Why further encourage some in the audience to suppose
that there is something "different" about the Jew and thereby
offer them a cheap excuse to intimate that the Jew invariably
"asks for it," sets himself up to be a victim and hence deserves
to be one? In fact, how far removed were my comments here
from those voices which even today declaim that European
Jewry ought to have physically resisted the Nazis, ought not to
have allowed themselves to go like "sheep to slaughter"? No, I
should not have referred to Memmi's analysis. The occasion
and place hardly called for critical remarks on the limitations of
some Jews. If anything, that audience needed to hear about the
executioners, not the victims.]

"How does my point relate to the younger generation here
and their so-called collective shame? Although a sense of shame
can be evidence that conscience is alive, carried to extremes this
feeling can disfigure the conscience, make of it a whipping dog
for masochistic self-indulgence. Not without cause has former
Prime Minister Ben-Gurion cautioned against misplaced and
misused guilt. In an interview with the German Press Agency
prior to the Eichmann trial, he said: 'We are all responsible for
our actions but we must not visit the crimes of the fathers upon
the children.' And the magnificent eighteenth chapter of Ezekiel
offers prophetic support for his position: 'The son shall not
suffer for the iniquity of the father, nor the father suffer for the
iniquity of the son; the righteousness of the righteous shall be
upon himself.' Again, the danger of misplaced guilt over the
atrocities has been accurately stated by Rabbi Harold Schulweis

in an article, 'Of Note: After Eichmann, What?' [*Commonweal,* January 19, 1962]: 'As essential as is the acknowledgment of responsibility and passive complicity for moral rehabilitation, its end will not be gained through a brooding guilt without direction. Surrounded with mirrors of the Hall of Horrors alone, the non-Jew will see himself as a grotesque figure. The danger lies in his subconscious acceptance of that reflection. The psychological process of internalizing the verdict passed upon his character and living up the role assigned him is not unfamiliar.' Similarly, referring to the shame that many Germans have about the recent past, Dr. Graf Schweinitz, of the Federal Press and Information Office in Bonn, at a reception last September for B'nai B'rith members making a visit to Germany, said: 'I think as long as shame exists there is also hope. However, no people in the world can live with the feeling of shame alone. Only he who esteems himself can esteem others. Germany can regain her self-esteem only in a spirit that combines atonement with dignity, with a feeling of being worthwhile.' "

[Is that why the German Press Information Office in Bonn, Amerika Haus officials, and some German newspapers, notably the *Frankfurter Allgemeine,* applauded the speech? Was I following their "line"? Specifically, a few days after the Frankfurt talk, the *Frankfurter Allgemeine* would publish—presently I shall touch on the history of this development—a translation of my remarks, capped by the headline: "Atonement with Dignity." These are the three words which the editorial staff had chosen to use as the signpost for their readers. I can hardly accuse this newspaper of foul play; obviously, some members of the editorial staff liked the talk enough to publish it. Nevertheless, atonement with dignity was not *the* thesis of my address. That title made it sound as though I were prescribing some sort of instant atonement—a clean new image in the eyes of the world, and this to be achieved without the exercise of moral sweat.]

"The words of Rabbi Schulweis and Dr. Schweinitz go right to the heart of the matter. I cannot envisage any possible good that would accrue, either individually or to humanity at large, if the younger generation here assumed a burden which was based on only guilt and shame. Whom would it help if they perpetually saw themselves as 'defendants'? Whom would it help if they beat their breasts and repeated in public that the Nazis were evil? Moreover, only those burdens *willingly* assumed, endured with *consent,* as the Talmud enjoins, by men who believe that despite the universal conditions of hate, terror, and murder, human life never ceases to have a deeply felt meaning, can call forth in them an ennobling transfiguration."

[This was the thesis of my speech—burdens *willingly* assumed with *consent.* But I understand now that I should have stated the thesis more emphatically and not merely settled for the stress placed on the two italicized words, assuming by this mechanical means that my auditors would know *where* the emphasis was intended. Indeed, it might have been far better if I had gone to the other extreme and said, boldly: Younger generation, stop whimpering, stop feeling sorry for yourselves. Like it or not, you *are* the sons of the murderers. Therefore assume— no, rather actively *choose* (as Sartre uses the term in discussing the necessity of each man's choosing his own identity and direction rather than having these imposed upon him by the whims of the historic moment)—the responsibilities of this onerous birthright.]

"Do we have any more moving modern-day examples of suffering 'endured with consent' than those pious Jews in Hitler's death camps who were consciously committed to the classic Jewish tradition of *kiddush ha-shem*—submissive martyrdom for the purpose of sanctifying the Name? They believed that every person should be respected because he is infused with a spark of the dignity of the Creator (there is a Hasidic saying that when man stoops low, God grows smaller, but when man stands upright, God is lifted on high); and they believed in being worthy of their suffering. Within the concentration camps, these saintly men went from hovel to hovel, comforting others, lifting up their courage, giving away their last piece of bread.

Going and coming from their places of inhuman labor, they would often lift up their voices in the song *Ani Maamin* ("I Believe"): 'I believe with perfect faith in the coming of the Messiah; and though he tarry, nonetheless do I believe!' And in the end they walked to their death, outwardly composed, inwardly resolute, perhaps remembering the words, 'Though He slay me, yet shall I follow Him!' "

[But was it wise to emphasize the spiritual resistance of these pious Jews and mention nothing about the physical resistance of, say, the Warsaw ghetto fighters? Shouldn't this audience have heard about Jews who defended themselves with arms rather than about those who were "submissive" at the moment of death? Further, is not the way these pious died the kind of ending that certain kinds of uninformed sentimentalists fancy that they would prefer for themselves? Perhaps something in them that may well once have responded with ardor to the destructive romanticism of Hitler now emotionally identified, for the wrong reasons, with the Jewish martyrs? Too bad, then, that I did not choose to stress the commitment of the ghetto fighters to the sanctity of Molotov cocktails and hand grenades.]

"And do we have more uplifting examples of moral obligations endured with consent than those thousands of Christian heroes in Europe who risked death to save Jews from becoming the victims of Hitler's Final Solution? In Berlin itself, many Jews lived to the end of the war, because courageous Christians passed them from home to home, from hiding place to hiding place. Denmark saved nearly its entire Jewish population. In Holland, some Dutch people arranged for a series of trains to take more than ten thousand Jewish children from Germany, Austria, and Czechoslovakia to England. There is the story of a German soldier stationed in Poland who repeatedly warned Jews of impending Gestapo raids and escorted Jewish laborers through the streets to their homes, to make certain they would not be molested. A German civilian contractor, Hermann Graebe, who now lives in Oakland, California, requisitioned Jews for work details and then established for them an underground escape route in the Ukraine. And Oskar Schindler, owner of a factory in Krakow, Poland, under the German occupation, by bribing the SS, had twelve hundred Jews classified as essential war workers in his factory, thus saving them from the concentration camps. There is the martyrdom of Father Maximilian Kolbe, a Polish priest in Auschwitz. And the heroic acts of Eduardo Focherini, editor of the Bologna *Catholic Daily,* who rescued scores of Jews. Righteous men, also, those ministers in Germany—Michael Cardinal Faulhaber, Bernard Lichtenberg, Pastor Dehnstads, Landesbischof Theophil Würm, Probst Heinrich Grueber, and Hermann Maas—who forcefully registered their protests against the destruction of European Jewry."

[Yes, but altogether there were so few of these brave spirits, so pitifully few, I should have added.]

"Let the deeds of these Jewish martyrs and Christian heroes serve as examples for the younger generation here. And as I believe that history may well have assigned to them the moral mandate of transforming collective guilt into constructive repentance, I should like to see them walk with humble hearts but upraised heads, assuming their burdens with 'consent.' If the Jewish people could rise up again from the crematories, it should be no less possible for them to be worthy of their burden as the descendants of a generation of killers.

"There remains the question: What are German students learning about Jewish history and anti-Semitism? By way of firsthand experience, I am not, of course in a position to say. Still, when I read through the wealth of information in two valuable books, *Education for Democracy in West Germany* and *The Politics of West Germany,* both edited by Walter Stahl, I am heartened to learn of the efforts to inform German youth on matters relating to the Jewish people. The presentation of Jewish history and the problems of anti-Semitism in both teacher-training programs and in the classrooms is receiving considerable attention; and there seems to be a growing amount of constructive critical thinking about the inadequate treatment of these subjects in German history textbooks. The Association of German Student Organizations has gone on record as recommending the establishment of a university institute for Jewish studies. The younger generation has been exposed to photographic exhibitions on the history and persecution of Jews and to such films as *Mein Kampf, The Diary of Anne Frank,* and *Night and Fog.* In the schools and universities, political education courses are placing stress on a critical examination of National Socialism and its racial theories. The press, radio, and TV have apparently done an impressive job in their treatment of the swastika epidemic of 1959, the trials of German war criminals, and in their presentation of material on the problems of Christian-Jewish understanding. These efforts constitute only a beginning, but, nevertheless, they would suggest that the prospects for the continuing education of the citizenry are favorable.

"Before coming to Germany, I had been advised by a friend that it would not be in good taste for me, as a Jew, to mention the concentration camps in public. Furthermore, it was his impression that Germans did not want to talk about the recent past, that for many Auschwitz was ancient history. Well, I can say that the students and young people I have come to know do not wish to enshroud this past in silence. They realize, as Dr. Schweinitz has put it, that 'unpleasant events aired in public are the price of freedom.' Their willingness to speak openly about these matters encourages me to be open with them. In sum, I feel that it is important for me to be here in the image and voice of an American-Jewish teacher. It is a unique opportunity to listen and to speak and to report to my friends in America and elsewhere who would like to believe in the German people again."

[An unfortunate conclusion. This implies *all* or most of the people of Germany, whereas I meant mainly the younger generation. But no excuses will do here. As a Jew speaking out on this subject, I was not free to violate the responsibility of being absolutely precise.]

Thus the speech. As I look back, what makes me especially uncomfortable is the apprehension that certain passages in the speech might have made German anti-Semites happy; for example, the reference to Memmi's the "Jew as a defendant" notion. There is also the possibility that some among those in the audience whose opinions did matter to me may have come away from the speech mistaking my motives. Did they wonder: "Whom is he trying to please?" "Does he feel that as a 'guest' in the land he has to say something flattering about his 'hosts'?" It would matter to me if I now knew for certain that these people believed that I had been used, seduced into whitewashing Germany's guilt.

But anyway, to move on now from the address to the various responses that it evoked. When I finished speaking, the audience applauded generously, and later Tam said that the talk had gone well. Yet neither of us was prepared for the first two questions. A young man, probably in his late twenties, stood up and asked, "Why do Jews think they're better than anyone else?" Just like that! Point blank, no qualifications, no hedging. His English was perfect, so I could not have misunderstood. Nor could one have misinterpreted the hostility in his voice. The audience was obviously stunned, embarrassed. Who the young man was I never found out. Afterward, he didn't attempt to speak with me, and I didn't feel the need to go looking for him. Tam has the impression that he left the hall shortly after asking his question.

What I said, in response to his provocation, is blacked out in my memory, and probably this is just as well. In replying, I remember trying to be factual, thoughtful, informative, as though he were an intellectual peer, when all the while my impulse was to leap from the lectern and nail him. At the least I should have challenged him by saying: "I'll try to answer your question if you'll first tell me why you asked it. Does the question come out of your personal observations? If so, would you care to share them with us?"

Right on the heels of his question and my fumbly response, a young woman, also in her late twenties (and again, like the young man before her, there was nothing about her appearance or manner to suggest that she was a crackpot), stood up and said, "Why are Jews so stubborn in discouraging Christians from marrying into the Jewish faith?" Her presumption was unmistakable—they are *wrong* to take that stand and must be publicly criticized for it.

I didn't see what her question, any more than the preceding one, had to do with my remarks, and I should have said that. Instead I tried to honor—and with no less ineptness than my previous response to the young man—what seemed to me, and still seems to me, an offensive question. I can't recall how I answered her. My sense is that I rambled and ended very wide of the mark. I remember thinking: For this I had come to Frankfurt! A rabbi, someone trained in Jewish history and Judaism, ought to be standing here, not me. But why so agitated, Herr Professor? Why such umbrage? After all, *you* elected to come to Frankfurt. What did you expect, a guarantee that you would have an entirely agreeable audience?

When I look back at this part of the Frankfurt experience, it does not seem strange that there would have been at least two openly hostile people in the audience. After all, in part I was scolding—though not nearly strongly or pointedly enough—the younger generation. You have insufficient reason for self-pity, I was, in effect, saying, so stop feeling sorry for yourselves. And even though this statement blurred, the listeners must have gotten the message. So why is it so surprising that some there should have resented being rebuked by a foreigner, an outsider?

Still, in subsequently presenting this same talk elsewhere in Germany, I not once encountered such unveiled hostility. Why then at Frankfurt? Did some special condition—e.g., the Frankfurt Auschwitz trial and its reverberations—obtain there that I was unaware of?

But I have given too much attention to this part of the Frankfurt talk. Actually, all the several questions that followed these two were pertinent and friendly. I said what there was to say in response to them, there was some more generous applause, and then the program was over.

It was only after I left the Amerika Haus that the thought occurred to me: Where were the Jewish members of the Society for Christian-Jewish Cooperation? It is true that after the address a member of the Amerika Haus staff introduced me to a couple of middle-aged people who *might* have been Jewish members of this organization, but he did not introduce—or at least I do not remember his doing so—them as such. Nonetheless, whether such members were present in the lecture hall or not, whether I was introduced to them afterward or not, the question remains—*why* didn't I ask after them? Wasn't I interested to meet these Jews? Or too keyed up in the aftermath of the talk to think about them? At the time it had not occurred to Tam either to seek out our sponsors. When we talked about this omission afterward, she said: "Maybe the reason is that neither of us can emotionally stomach the fact that Jews, by their own choice, still live in Germany. So we may have unconsciously preferred not to meet them."

Well, whatever the explanation, these "cosponsors" of the address remain for us silent, invisible Jews.

The speech was not to have a one-shot career. A reporter from the *Frankfurter Allgemeine,* one of Germany's most influential and respected newspapers (*The New York Times* of Germany, a number of people said to me), was in the audience, and the next day the address got a favorable review. Then one of the paper's editors got a copy of the talk from an Amerika Haus official; and, in short, the address, translated into German by someone on the editorial staff, appeared in the March 25, 1964 issue. A director of the Frankfurt Amerika Haus called me in Nuremberg to say how pleased he and his colleagues were; this was the first time, he said, that the *Frankfurter Allgemeine* had ever published, in its entirety, a speech delivered at an Amerika Haus. "It's a remarkable, very unusual thing for them to do. They're very selective about what they print," he said. Then the young German connected with the American Embassy in Bonn phoned to say how happy he was at seeing the talk in print, and that the Frankfurt Amerika Haus director reported to him the strong effect it had had on the audience. He too stressed how rare it was for the *Frankfurter Allgemeine* to have printed the address. And he accurately predicted that I would receive many invitations for speaking engagements.

Some other repercussions? Apparently someone from the *Amerika Haüser* sent press releases on the talk to both German and American newspapers. In any event, clippings from the former were sent to me by an official of the Frankfurt Amerika Haus. One writer contrasted the playwright Arthur Miller and the American-Jewish professor, Halperin. He was the bad guy, I the good one. Evidently, Miller had been an observer at the Frankfurt trial of the former Auschwitz guards and was quoted as making some sharply critical comments on the conduct of the trial. The writer argued that Miller's critique was inaccurate and unwarranted, that the trials were accomplishing a good deal, etc. In contrast, here was the "humble" and "humane" Herr Halperin speaking perceptively and wisely at the Amerika Haus. I was not flattered. Better that the writer of this story should have had warrant to write me off as a bad ("bad" Jew?) guy.

Then San Francisco friends forwarded clippings from three papers, *The New York Times,* the *San Francisco Examiner,* and the *San Francisco Call Bulletin,* all of which had printed reports on the Frankfurt talk. *The New York Times* piece, carrying an April 3d by-line story by Arthur J. Olsen, dated Bonn, March 31, and referring to the talk in the larger context of the Frankfurt trial, emphasized my analogy between the young American Jews I had known in the '30s and the temper of some young people I had met in Germany.

> An American exchange teacher, Prof. Irving Halperin of San Francisco State College, who is lecturing at Erlangen University, has noted parallels between the state of mind of West German students now and that of young American Jews in the nineteen-thirties.
>
> In a recent lecture he described his students as bewildered at being "cold-shouldered" by other Europeans

or at being called on to answer for deeds they know of only from history books.

"They believe they are discriminated against because they are Germans," Professor Halperin said, "just as in the nineteen-thirties many of us believed—and often not on good grounds—that we were handicapped in competition for certain positions or seeking admission to certain professional or social organizations because we were Jews."

The "and often not on good grounds" is not, alas, what appeared in my Frankfurt address. What I did say was "—more often than not with good reason—"

But to return to the *Frankfurter Allgemeine* publication of the speech, readers of that issue shortly thereafter responded with letters, which were forwarded to my mailing address at the University of Erlangen. One correspondent, probably middle-aged, was certain that the address would not influence German youth, adding that the Jews killed Christ, and this was justification enough for what, in turn, was done to them. Then there was a hate letter from a man which opened and closed on the loving note that "you and your friends" haven't learned from what happened to you; "you and your friends" will find that you can't poison our youth; "you and your friends" are going to get it again someday soon."

Then there was the correspondent who stated that Germans were no better or worse than other peoples; that in some places of the world similar war-crimes trials were soft-pedaled but here they were dramatized. Also, he insisted that many of the defendants involved in the war-crimes trial at Frankfurt were reasonable, decent people, not criminals. "Let's forget these trials," he concluded. "They only feed into East German Communist propaganda, anyway. Besides, the defendants did what they *had* to; they were under orders. Anyone would have done the same."

One of the more thoughtful correspondents was a Budapest Jew who wrote to say that his wife, children, and thirty-one relatives had died during the Holocaust. And this was the past I wanted him to forget. What could I say to that man? Two or three times I started a letter to him, but the words stuck in my throat.

"You were a little too easy on the Germans," a middle-aged Jew in Fürth said to me shortly after the speech appeared in the *Frankfurter Allgemeine*. He and his wife had been in concentration camps. After I explained what my intent had been, he said caustically: "You want to keep it fifty-fifty. Half to blame and half to forgive?" I said that, if anything, the ratio was closer to 75 percent blame and 25 percent "forgive." "Well, it can't be done," he said. "After the war, in 1946, you couldn't find one bad German. Not one. They swore they were good to Jews. Yes, any German who had given a Jew a cigarette during the war claimed he was a friend of the Jews."

Rabbi Schulweis, whom I had cited in the talk, saw it as a philosophical appreciation of the difficulties confronting Jews and Christians about the "unmastered past." The director of the Fulbright Commission in Germany wrote to say that he had rarely seen a statement on this subject that went to the heart of the matter as did my article. He was especially pleased that it had done justice to the efforts of the younger generation in Germany to assume the burden of collective shame. He warned that many people would probably misunderstand my intention in presenting the talk, but that I was not to feel offended or disappointed. He was confident that my views would be shared by most young educated Germans.

Several days after the Frankfurt talk, I gave the same address at the Amerika Haus in Nuremberg. Many in the audience were smarting from an attack on Germany's younger generation by Martha Gellhorn in a *Harper's* article, "Is There a New Germany?" (February, 1964). (In brief, Miss Gellhorn had asserted that there was no "new Germany," and that the younger generation probably did not have the "guts and imagination" to help create one.)

"We're paying reparations to the Jewish people and to

Israel," one young man said after I had finished speaking. Then, as though taking a hint from the visibly embarrassed audience reaction to his remark, he quickly added: "But of course this is no excuse for what happened. Money can't make up for it." Then another young man said bluntly: "The government's policy is to be nice toward Jews. But we don't really feel sorry for them. First of all, we never see any here to feel sorry for. And also, we just have too many things on our minds—how to get a college degree, a good job, and save enough money to buy a car." Another young man, originally from the East German zone, related how his parents would often say to him that there were too many rich Jews in Germany and that their power had to be diminished. He himself had never put any credence in this charge. What now specifically concerned him was the question of what is Germany doing to become truly democratic. And here he was of the opinion that all too many were making dangerous compromises with their political freedom. A sophisticated young woman said: "I was moved by what you said, but I don't feel guilty. I can look you straight in the eyes. When the main synagogue of our town was burned down by the Nazis, my father called together his friends to see what he could do about rebuilding it. Of course he was warned not to meddle. Anyone who knew him can tell you that he was a friend of the Jews, and he did what he could to help them. At the end of the war he died in an Allied prisoner of war camp."

Someone else, who later would confess to me that he had been a member of Hitler's youth organization, said that I had been much too optimistic about German youth. Specifically, I had not taken into account—probably because of lack of contact with them—the pernicious influence of reactionary student fraternities and dueling societies, which, in his opinion, were the strongholds of ultraright nationalism.

Then there was the middle-aged woman who said in a heartfelt but nevertheless bumbling manner: "Many of us today may think we had nothing to do with what happened to the Jews. But some of us saw certain things—like Jews being rounded up.

Perhaps others hadn't wanted to know what was happening to them. But now I honestly can't remember how much we knew or what we could have done about it. . . . Besides, what could we have done to save Jews when even listening to foreign broadcasts in our own homes could mean death?"

To an extent, what this woman said coincides with the remarks made by Rolf Hochhuth during an interview in 1964 (E. R. Bentley, ed., *The Storm Over The Deputy;* Grove Press, Inc., 1964). Recalling what the German populace had heard concerning mass shootings of Jews from soldiers returning from Russia, Hochhuth said:

> We thought it could not be true. . . . It was so ugly and brutal. But in a war, people's feelings become insensitive. The Jews had disappeared from our lives but we knew from books and school lessons that Jews were described as *untermenschen* and that all other people were second class. We also knew that the Russian prisoners of war were treated badly and died of starvation, but this didn't affect one; each one had his own problems; we trembled for members of our own families. (P. 47.)

In short, each person had his own problems, so who could be too concerned about what was happening to the *Untermenschen*? But the difference between the woman in Nuremberg and Hochhuth is that the latter has not shirked the necessity of taking a hard look at what took place during the nightmare of Hitler's Germany; and he seeks to understand himself as a German within the perspective of that tragic history. Moreover, there *is* an answer to the Nuremberg woman's question—"What could we have done?" Some Germans *did* speak up in protest against the persecution of Jews. Provost Bernard Lichtenberg, for one, cried out against the burning of synagogues:

> What took place yesterday we know; what will be tomorrow we do not know; but what happens today, this

we have witnessed; outside [this church] the synagogue
is burning, and that is also a house of God.

And in the spring of 1942, students at the University of Munich
distributed leaflets protesting the mass killings of Jews in Poland
and criticizing the German people for being indifferent in the
face of these crimes. Sophie and Hans Scholl were executed for
their part in this demonstration.

Thinking back now on the Nuremberg woman's question—
What could we have done?—I remember what Professor Karl
Jaspers has written: "When the Jews were being transported,
we did not go to the streets and cry out until they destroyed us
too. . . . We are to blame that we are still alive." And a member of the Bundestag, Adolf Arndt, speaking to Germans, said:
"I have to tell you that I know that I share the guilt. I did not
go in the streets and shout aloud when I saw them driving the
Jews away by the truck-load. I did not put on the Yellow Star
myself and say, 'Take me too!'" Or as the historian Golo
Mann has written, "If we are to be exact about the guilt, one
half of our nation would have to sit as judges of the other half."
I remember too Albert Schweitzer's response when he was
asked the same question—"You can speak out."

When this woman had finished speaking, I said: "Had it ever
occurred to you during those years to walk up to a Jew wearing
a yellow star and say this to him: 'Look, there's nothing I can
do to help you, because this would mean my life and the lives of
my family. But I want you to know that what my country is
doing to your people is criminal, and I deplore it'? Certainly
these words wouldn't have saved the life of that Jew, but at least
they would have let him know that there were sympathetic
Germans."

"Yes . . . yes I see," she replied, as though suddenly moved
by a recognition that much could have been done.

On leaving the Nuremberg Amerika Haus that evening, one
young man reportedly muttered his indignation to a young lady,
who later became a friend of Tam's and mine. "They come over
here and preach to us," he angrily complained. "The Jews! I'm

sick of them and the war trials and of hearing that Germany did this and Germany did that. Why don't they tend to their own business?"

Several weeks after this occasion, I gave the same address in Berlin, Hamburg, and the University of Göttingen. At the Berlin Amerika Haus, I was stunned to see Probst Heinrich Grueber in the first row. I knew that his place of work was in the Berlin area, but it never would have occurred to me that he would have wanted to hear the address. The presence of this man who had been in Dachau mocked my academician's stance behind the lectern. . . . Afterward, he said something kind about the talk and added that it was important for Jews like myself to be in Germany.

As I was leaving the lecture hall, a middle-aged woman came over and declared, with strong feeling, that she had nothing but contempt for those Germans who felt sorry for themselves simply because they were unpopular in some parts of the world. An elderly man standing beside her said he had been in the camps and that I had spoken well. And several other people indicated that they found the address meaningful.

Weeks later, a letter came to me from a German Jew, himself a victim of the Hitler years, who had heard the address in Berlin. At the time he had taken exception to my views but had decided that it would have been indelicate if another Jew should have risen to oppose the speaker. He seemed convinced that the moral-philosophical speculations I expressed in the address were made in all good faith; nevertheless, they were based, he argued, on completely incorrect premises. But let his own words speak for him:

Of course this "German reality" presents itself in a quite different light from the reality of any number of Jews in their daily encounters and experiences here. For he, the Fulbright professor protected by prestige, passport, and other privileges, encounters these realities at best only after a filtering process but never directly.

Moreover, it becomes serious if these very limited, un-
critical insights imply that there are two alternatives—
either hating or not hating the Germans for what happened. It becomes more dangerous when those who were
the victims are not asked about their views. Certainly
fine monologues should be made, but have you, Professor Halperin, gathered enough experiences to present
your views as representatively "Jewish"? Would you
maintain that your exceptional situation is in any way
comparable with that of any number of anonymous Jews
in Germany? I am afraid that you are giving yourself
up to theoretically seductive but dangerous illusions. To
quote Brecht—"The circumstances they are not so."

His letter left me feeling uncomfortable on a number of
counts. What did I know about the day-to-day life of German
Jewry? One afternoon I had briefly observed, at a distance,
some of their faces in the Berlin Jewish Community Center located near the Kurfürstendamm. To my eyes these Jews appeared fugitive, ghostlike, and I could not understand how they
could go on living in Germany. Also, my correspondent was
right in saying that it was easy for an American professor, protected by the privileges of a "guest," to speak up as a self-
identified Jew in Germany. Would I have had the courage to deliver the same kind of public address had I been one of the
"anonymous" Jews of Germany? Certainly my correspondent
did not believe that an "anonymous" German Jew, lacking
"protection," could speak his mind out on the controversial
question of collective shame without facing subtle forms of cen-
sure from the non-Jewish community. And perhaps, too, he had
accurately predicted that the address would be misunderstood
as posing easy alternatives for Jews and offering "instant redemption" for Germans. Since then I have often thought about
his letter; it increasingly makes sense.

In Hamburg I spoke at the invitation of Pastor John Joachim
Ziegenrücker of the Evangelische Akademie. Afterward, what
especially pleased me was the way in which the pastor, a very

attractive individual, said tersely, "We've heard you speak and now we must go to work." I am certain he did.

What troubled me that evening were the eyes of a Jew from Hamburg, a leading member of the local Christian-Jewish Cooperation Society, which had cosponsored the address. Just prior to taking a train back to Nuremberg, I sat across from him in the restaurant of the railroad station. His eyes looked at me through depths of suffering and humanity and calm understanding. "I wish you could stay on a while, so we could talk," he said to me. Clearly, he felt I did not grasp too well what was needed in Germany in the way of efforts from both Germans and Jews. I could see my role through his eyes. Here I had come to speak to people like himself who had directly experienced the Holocaust. What arrogance! And yet, wouldn't it have been extremely difficult for a German Jew like himself to have spoken on the same topic? Whereas coming from the American "professor," the talk was given a veneer of intellectual "objectivity."

Following the conclusion of the address at the University of Göttingen, a young man in the audience said he was convinced that only individual Germans confronting individual Jews could help to heal the wounds of the past; in his opinion, addresses before public audiences would not be too effective. And a young lady made an impassioned plea for "just accepting Jews as other people—neither feeling sorry for nor bending over backward to be nice to them."

So now the speeches were over, and on returning to Nuremberg and looking back, I would attempt to assess the various responses to them. The letter from the Jew in Berlin who believed that I did not at all see the day-to-day situation in Germany continued to trouble me. On the other hand there was the phone call I got from an Amerika Haus official in Göttingen. He was phoning, he said, not in an official but rather private capacity, to indicate again how pleased he had been with the address. "I am glad you spoke here. We meet so few Jews."

Looking back now, I can only dimly recall a few of the faces from among the audiences in Frankfurt, Nuremberg, Berlin, Hamburg, the University of Göttingen. They come back to me, those faces, distant and indefinite as images in dreams. Sometimes they appear accusatory, sometimes pitying, almost always troubled. And more vivid and unsettling than the rest is the face of the Jew from Frankfurt who wanted to tell me something.

10

DACHAU: 1964

IT IS ALL VERY FLATTERING to be the Herr American Professor on a generously sponsored lecture tour in Germany. You arrive at a railroad depot or airport and are met by a luxurious chauffeur-driven limousine dispatched by the local Amerika Haus. Then you are driven to the place where the talk is to be given and later you are driven back to the place of departure. In between your arrival and departure, officials fuss over you, generously cater to your every request, introduce you to local celebrities. In short, attention is lavished on you in a manner you are unaccustomed to as an academic in America. Now add to this VIP treatment the special circumstances of my being a Jew and speaking on a "sensitive" topic, and it seemed to me that sometimes my hosts in various cities were excessively obliging. In any case, there is no denying that, as my German Jewish correspondent from Berlin had written in his letter, I was neatly cellophaned and protected by a "privileged" status.

Until a day comes when something in you cries out: My God, did it really all happen here—Crystal Night, the burning of synagogues, the camps? And if it did happen here, *where* are the physical reminders of the recent past? Has *everything* been perfumed and painted over? Where are the palpable vestiges of the recent past? I had spoken abstractly about the Holocaust in lecture halls, and now I had the need to *see* it.

So in mid-April I visited Dachau. I came there sans a

chauffeur-driven car, sans the services of a reception committee or obliging hosts. This visit marked the fourth and final phase of our stay in Germany.

"Hier Dachau," a gruff voice sounded over a loudspeaker system in the station. Twenty years ago, they who were brought to Dachau in transports would have trembled on hearing the name. Through openings in the cattle cars they would have searched out the horizons for the buildings of the dreaded camp. But on the day of my arrival, all I could see in the station were a number of flattop cars bearing new automobiles for delivery. Less than twenty years after the gates of the camps were flung open, Germany was enjoying the fruits of prosperity. And twenty years later, with impunity, I, a Jew, could choose to take a public bus to the former camp. There was a return ticket to Munich in my wallet. In short, no risks.

The morning was gray and drizzly. This was just as well. In Dachau I would not want to see a bright sky. The houses and stores of the street directly across from the station looked drab and pinched. Perhaps it was the gray sky that made them appear oppressive, as though the town were weighed down by a curse. A one-legged man on crutches hopped over cobblestones. The war, I guessed. One of the thousands of Germany's crippled war survivors. In this place, I did not feel pity for such cripples.

From a bus moving toward the eastern end of the town, I observed the people in the passing streets. Didn't they know? I heard an inner voice. Did they care? What did they see, hear, feel when the prisoners were led through the town? How many said to themselves: Why should I stick my neck out for those Jews? How many spoke out in protest?

The former camp is at the end of the bus line. Surprisingly, the barracks, some thirty of them, and grounds comprise a rather small area—990 feet wide and 200 feet long. I had pictured that Hell would be endless; "the Planet Dachau," some survivors speak of it.

Dachau? Where now the roll call square? The infirmary

where the medical experiments were performed? The mortuary? Barracks 15, where the Jews were held? The barracks that held Dean Grueber? Rabbi Shapiro? The mass graves? The prisoners with staring, sunken eyes? In fact, *what* is to be seen at Dachau?

All that I could see was the main street—"The Street of Liberty," as the prisoners ironically referred to it—lined on either side by tall, beautiful trees of equal height. And behind the trees were dun, scaly barracks; equispaced, equisized, monotonously alike—as indistinguishable as mounds of corpses.

Refugees from eastern countries, come to Germany to share the fruits of prosperity, were living in them. How much did they know about what had taken place in the rooms they now occupied?

Children were playing in the main streets and the spaces between the barracks, in places where twenty years before blood had run.

What is a visitor supposed to *feel?* An inferno was here, it is gone. Silenced are the cries of prisoners. Did I not know this was Dachau, these barracks and streets would make no special claims on my eyes.

I did not know what I expected to find there.

The Memorial Chapel is round, towerlike, forty-one feet high, built of unhewn rocks, above its entrance an immense crown of thorns. It stands where once the infamous roll call square was. As I approached the monument, some building and grounds workers were mowing a lawn before it. The fragrance of freshly cut grass, I thought, dryly. Not at all like the smell of burning human flesh.

From the chapel's ceiling is suspended a cross, and a sculptured figure of Christ is on it. Yet it is not his figure that ought to be up there but rather a Jew who had died six million times over.

The ironic juxtapositions of history: first, the crematoria, and then, twenty years later, on the same ground, a tower of remembrance. Germans had built both, in a cycle of murder and atonement.

Inside the chapel were wreaths of flowers. Should there have been? Wouldn't it have been more appropriate for the starkly austere rock walls to be without them? Because Dachau is not a place for ever-returning spring, not a place for flowers as a symbol of resurrection. The dead are silent and will not return again. . . .

A sign indicated the entrance to the Camp Museum, where the exhibits and crematoria are. A chubby young American with a mamma's boy face stood before the entrance to the small building in which the old crematorium was housed. He was energetically clicking away on an elaborate-looking camera. Why *feel* when you can peep and click? The omnipresent camera-eye of our time even here, in Dachau. For a moment I felt something close to anger. You take that camera out of here! I almost told him. What was he going to do with those pictures—prove to somebody that *he* was here? That he saw "all those terrible things"?

But the trouble is that I might have said the same thing in spades about myself. What was the substantial difference between his camera and my literary interest in Dachau?

In the museums are exhibition cases, documents, photographs, data, statistics. A whip used for beating the prisoners is under glass. Also under glass is a dingy, striped blue and white uniform, the one worn by the prisoners. Wall charts list how many died from illness, from medical experiments, from hanging. There is even a breakdown of how much profit the SS realized from the slave labor, clothes, jewelry, gold teeth, hair and bone pulp of the average prisoner. Altogether, it is as though everything had been cataloged and arranged to prove to even the most skeptical that Dachau *was,* that its much publicized horrors have not been exaggerated.

I walked past the exhibition cases and charts feeling neither grief nor horror. The question occurred to me then and it returns to me now: Is it appropriate for a museum to be at Dachau, a museum displaying prisoners' uniforms, charts, statistics? Rather it seems to me that in such a place, where the ovens were, the visitor ought to confront empty rooms and silence—a silence in which one might reflect on what he knows, even at second remove, from having read the literature of the Holocaust and from having spoken with survivors of their day-to-day existence in the hell of Dachau and other concentration camps.

Are statistics and exhibit cases necessary if one has already heard a survivor relate how on several occasions she was forced to kneel on the ground for hours at a time while holding outstretched a brick in either hand? What are the "facts" beside her account of how she saw a female guard calmly shoot a starving woman prisoner for rifling some spoiled food from a garbage can? Will the charts and figures tell how it was to be starving and daydreaming of how a single biscuit would taste? Or how it feels for a new prisoner to have all of her hair shaved off and then to laugh hysterically on seeing how bizarre her bald pate appears in a mirror? The printed information under a glass case will not sufficiently explain why a former sculptress from Prague chose to use her bread rations for making figurines. (She was still making figurines out of bread when they came to take her off to the gas chambers.) And does one need to hear the "vital statistics" cited after hearing a survivor incriminate herself: "Maybe I should have put some reddish brick on the cheeks of my little sister. Maybe that would have helped her to get through the selection"?

Sightless before exhibit cases, I wondered how many yards from there Probst Grueber had stood when his teeth were knocked out by a guard and when he rose from the ground to say to the other, "I don't hate you"?

Should a museum be at Dachau?

There are no facts or figures on the number of times prisoners, starving and desperate to stay alive, had stolen bread from their friends, the helpless and sick, and even their own parents. No figures exist on the squashed babies which were carried out, feet first, from deportation train cars. No photographs are available of the food rotting on the bunks of the dying and dead. Or of a small child wheeling a doll in a baby

buggy toward the gas chambers. We have no phonograph recordings of pious Jews lifting their voices in the song *Ani
Maamin* ("I Believe"). "I believe with perfect faith in the coming of the Messiah; and though he tarry, nonetheless do I
believe!" No recordings of saintly men going from hut to hut
lifting up the morale of their fellow sufferers, encouraging those
who were near the breaking point to hold on. Or the questions
of children who could not understand why God was letting Hitler throw people into furnaces. Nothing to recapture the stink of
dysentery from bloated, rotting bodies which very likely once
filled the rooms of this building.

Should a museum be at Dachau?

Next door to the room containing the exhibition cases was
the gas chamber. I could neither visualize several hundred
bodies standing inside it nor picture the gas descending and
spreading out from overhead vats, over a mound of still bodies.
How imagine the few, the strongest, clawing their way to the
top of the mound, there thrashing about frantically, uselessly,
for air? I could not picture pious men, in the last seconds of
consciousness, uttering the words of the prayer *Shema*—"Hear,
O Israel: the Lord our God is one Lord."

I left the chamber and stepped into a large, high-ceilinged
room containing four ovens. At the foot of these were wreaths
of flowers. Flowers! I could not understand that. Yes, flowers
placed on the earth, beside tombs, can be a gesture of respect
for the dead. But beside these ovens!

And there were other picture takers here, energetically clicking away at the ovens. And the technicians were there also. An
American, in a lifeless, matter-of-fact tone, as though describing
the process of mining salt, was carefully explaining to his companions the chronology of the entire operation, from the inser-
tion of the corpses into the ovens to the disposal of the ashes.
Clearly, the technical ingenuity and efficiency of the oven
mechanism greatly impressed these two visitors from America.
All praise to Third Reich efficiency.

In the last room is an outsized autograph-style book in which

visitors are invited to record their impressions and sentiments.
Just like that. Impressions hurried onto paper and recorded for
all posterity. I turned the pages. The inscriptions in English are
not lacking in the canned clichés on the Holocaust: How awful!
We must not forget! How could such a thing happen? I shall
never forgive the Germans. God forgive them, for they know
not what they did. The capacity for barbarism is in all of us.
Hitler was an evil man. . . .

I had nothing to enter into this Book of Impressions.

A light rain was falling as I left the museum. It concerned me
that I had felt so little sorrow while going from place to place in
Dachau. Some visitors had been able to weep before the ovens.
Others looked as though they were thinking, "This, this is a tremendous experience!" Why, then, was I so numbed? All those
books on the Holocaust which I had read, but now Dachau
struck me as unreal—a wax museum. The bones of the dead
were invisible under the earth: mounds of anonymous, undif-
ferentiated and unclassified, bones. . . .

On the way back to the bus stop, I again passed the
Memorial Chapel. Once more I did not feel that Christ ought to
be up there on a cross. Why not the figure of someone like
Rabbi Shapiro of Fürth who had endured the Golgotha of Dachau guards, work details, freezing winters? The Nazis had broken his body and tried to desecrate his spirit. But despite his
own private sorrows, the death of his wife and children, the loss
of his homeland, in Dachau he sought to "lift up" his fellow
sufferers in the camp. So if Christ was up on the cross in the
Chapel, why not also a figure symbolizing the anguish and spiritual achievement of such a pious Jew?

I went slowly through the treelined main street observing, as
though from a vast distance, the deserted, ghostlike watchtowers
and rusted barbed-wire fence and wall defining the boundaries
of the former camp. The air was still. The cries of women had
once been heard here. At night, eerie red lamps had lighted the
walls, and beside the barbed wire the shadows of prisoners had
moved like apparitions in a nightmare. Inside the narrow huts,

the prisoners had slumped down on the floor or on their bunks, bread rations in hand. Outside, the sky, distant and silent, had moved indifferently over Dachau.

Just as I was approaching an exit gate and the bus stop beyond, a little boy appeared on a bicycle, stopped directly in front of me, touched my hand, and chirped out the familiar salutation, *"Grüss Gott,"* and continued on. This he did quite easily, freely. His hand was warmly alive. I thought of Sigi Baier, of his not even having understood the word *Yid*—and then, by extension, of German elementary school children, for whom the name Hitler is synonymous with boogie man. I wanted to believe in the young of Germany. . . .

The boy on the bicycle rode off. Long after leaving Dachau, I still heard his voice.

II

DEPARTURE

AFTER DACHAU, the remaining three months of our stay in Germany were as a postscript. Spring came on a still, gentle Saturday morning; buds flowered on the plum tree. Transformed into gardeners, the children watered the lawn and flowers. Dan's trousers and then Jon's were soon caked with mud. From time to time they put down the hose to dig for worms.

Birds rested within the trees. In one, a robin was building a nest. Frau Baier said that each spring the same bird returned to the same tree. The children watched the robin converting straw and twigs into a home.

Upstairs, Sigi played the accordion, offering music to the benign air.

In the small gardens beyond the end of the street, elderly people were bent over spades and hoes.

War, genocide, legless men, and then another cycle of rain, sun, and growth.

One summer morning our three children ascend step ladders to pick cherries from a tree in the backyard. Sitting on one of its upper branches, the gray of her hair showing through the leaves, the pockets of her smock bulging with cherries, Frau Baier instructs them in the lore of knowing which ones to pick. Perched on the ladders, our city-bred children are pleased with themselves. They will not easily forget *their* Frau Baier. In their memories *she* will be Germany, and they will have to balance their fondness for her against the accounts that they will hear about Germans who murdered Jews.

In the backyard on a hot afternoon, Frau Baier filled an immense washtub with cold water and seated all three kids in it. She wore a bathing suit, they nothing. Tam and I stood before a window on the third floor.

The kids sat one behind the other, as though they were ready to sail out to sea in a tub. Grinning impishly, Frau Baier turned the hose on them. *"Wasser! Wasser!"* she chirped. Water pelted the kids. They and she shrieked with laughter. The game was on. They tried, unsuccessfully, to dodge the sprayed water by ducking their heads below the rim of the tub. Finally, Dan, desperately taking the offensive, left the tub, wrenched the hose away from Frau Baier, and began to sprinkle her. Dina and Jon joined forces with him, and they took turns at the hose, deluging the good woman while she romped wildly around the yard, pretending to flee from the water and all the while howling with laughter. After a while she said, *"Genug* (enough),*"* and the kids, putting down the hose, congratulated one another. As the price for her surrender, she brought the victors a dish of delicious homemade *Lebkuchen* (gingerbread cookies, a Nuremberg specialty).

Several miles away, within a bleak tenementlike building on a Fürth street, a minyan of orthodox Jews conduct Sabbath morning services. Rabbi Shapiro sways, chants prayers in a strong, clear voice. After all that he has been through, where does he get the strength to pray with such vigor and devotion? I, looking on, wonder. Clad in prayer shawls, the congregants face east, into the windows of a house occupied by non-Jews. What do they make of this small number of Jews who pray in the building across the way? Do they ever wish that those "outsiders" from Eastern European countries would go away, disappear, like a bad dream? Were any of them distressed on the night that the three-hundred-year-old synagogue of Fürth was burned down and the city's Jews "went away"?

In the sparsely furnished cold rooms of this building, they

know how to honor the Sabbath with fervor. Women with kind eyes and warm voices serve a fine Sabbath meal of homemade bread, red wine, chopped onions and eggs, soup, gefilte fish, a roast, and applesauce. Afterward, the families sing Sabbath songs; the children play games. On Sabbath no one speaks about the concentration camps, the loss of family members, though sometimes they reminisce on the old days, before Hitler, in Praga, Vilna, Lodz, Warsaw. The fathers read the first benedictions with ardor; the children are marvelously affectionate with one another. Outside this tenement the place is affluent postwar Germany. Inside these cold rooms are human warmth and love and the joy of the Sabbath.

Miraculously, the Jewish people still live—even in Fürth.

Walkers enter and leave the woods as we sit in the sun drinking coffee. Before us swans and mallards drift back and forth over the pond. Waiters in bright-green lederhosen move from table to table. The patrons are smartly and prosperously dressed. This outdoor café is located beside one of Nuremberg's forest preserves and not far from Dutzendteich. A country of walkers, I muse, seeing middle-aged and elderly people embark upon trails leading into the woods.

The Baiers sit across from us. We have persuaded them to be our guests at this café. I say persuaded because at first Frau Baier was reluctant to go there. She rightfully prides herself on making better coffee and pastry than can be gotten at a café, any café. "So why not come to our place?" she had urged. "That's much better than to spend your money for ersatz."

Now the Baiers speak of their favorite places in the country. She is particularly ecstatic about a town where her relatives live. *"Die Luft ist schön!"* she exclaims. Like champagne. *"Und das Essen ist prima!"* She suggests that some weekend we all drive there, that her relatives would be pleased to meet us.

But when it is not possible to get away to the country, Herr Baier says, following the thread of the conversation, it is important to walk. It is not good to sit all day long. He has earned the right to say this. In addition to being a zealous walker, he is a dedicated bicyclist. Whenever the weather permits, he bicycles to and from his place of work, a distance of several miles. It is better, he contends, than to sit in streetcars. The man is in superb physical condition; the movements of his lean and wiry body are as fluid and supple as those of a man twenty years his junior.

I would like to go to Paris and Rome, he says, after Tam and I discuss a projected trip to France and Italy. He has not done too much traveling, but still, his is a rich talent for living at home. Clearly, he derives his satisfactions from the everyday phenomena of the immediate physical world that lie around him: his workshop in the basement, the back and front yards, his handiwork around the house.

Frau Baier and he especially enjoy walking in the magnificent woods that encircle Nuremberg. In them they feel free and can walk and think without interruption from the usual distractions of the city. I can picture them walking along a path, concentrating on whatever they are seeing and not restless, as is characteristic of young people, to look around for the next thing.

When I mention how in the United States there are constant struggles by those who seek to preserve the dwindling natural wilderness areas for hikers, they shake their heads. It is difficult for them to grasp why roads had to be made for the convenience of those who no longer care to walk. In Nuremberg such excessive pampering of motorists would be unthinkable. Were they that dedicated to other kinds of preservation twenty years before?

In all the time we lived in their house, we did not press the Baiers for their views on Hitler and the Third Reich; neither Tam nor I felt we had a right to put them on the spot by posing leading questions. However, once, in passing, of her own volition, Frau Baier did say (she, the kids, and I were strolling through the magnificent Nuremberg zoo at the time) that even though Hitler had accomplished some good things—for example, the building of this zoo—he was bad for Germans and the country. This was said with evident sincerity, but I sensed that, understandably, she wasn't telling me all that she felt about the past. Obviously, we would prefer to think that the Baiers never consciously contributed to the oppression of a single Jew. I cannot imagine that they ever did. And yet, when the Führer promised the Nuremberg populace he would build bigger and better autobahns and drive criminals from the streets, did the Baiers applaud—and go on walking in the woods?

Not that a love of nature and obeisance to tyrannical leaders are contradictory or mutually exclusive impulses. Hitler was said to be a devotee of mountains and forests. There is a photograph I have seen of this destructive Pied Piper sitting on a large boulder, in some green mountain setting near Berchtesgaden, looking dreamily, tranquilly, off into space. His face appears suffused with light, as though he were in some sort of trance. One can imagine the romantic music of Wagner's *Siegfried Idyll* tremulously sounding in his ears. Rhetoric about the purity and spiritual wholesomeness of nature rolls in his head. To our retrospective eyes his face has a semblance of Edgar Allan Poe's demented look. But to loyal Germans of the Third Reich, in the moment that this photograph was taken, Hitler could readily appear as a poetic soul attuned to the Platonic forms of cliffs and woods.

The trouble is that he will not long repose on that rock. Soon he will arise with a rage-inflamed face and shake his fists at the sky, cursing F. D. R., Churchill, and world Jewry for Germany's increasing military defeats. Silent, he may pass for the possessed poet, but the strident voice is that of Cain. . . .

Swans and mallards drift by, the sounds of conversation from adjoining tables are almost melodious, walkers continue to enter and emerge from the woods. Less than a mile from this bucolic retreat are the moldering ruins of the never completed World Congress Building, in which Hitler had planned—or so I had heard—to imprison F. D. R., Churchill, and other leaders of the defeated countries. Yes, the Leader had had great expectations for the thousand years of the Third Reich. Always he went in the direction exclusively pointed out to him by "Destiny"! "I go the way fate has pointed me as assuredly as a man walking in his sleep," he once said.

But these walkers in the near distance, what special "destiny" is it they look to as they move beside trees? Who is it that they wish to conquer? What will to power is involved in their modest observations of flora and fauna? Rather, I picture them walking with their senses open to that which exists directly before and around them. One cannot imagine them facelessly goose-stepping along paths, effecting blitzkreig en route to the East. Each walker, sauntering through the woods, has chosen the liberty of solitude. I observe no connection between the faceless goose-stepper of the Third Reich and the relaxed, ambling gait of the hikers over this sylvan landscape. The latter, having given of themselves to the common, unheroic pleasures of the physical world, emerge from the woods looking content and benign.

Toward the end of our stay in the café, Frau Baier recalls how as a young girl she and her friends would bicycle away from the city and along the highway to the bottom of some *Berg* (mountain) and go hiking. Later they would swim in ice-cold streams. Ah, those were the days. . . .

"Soon we will give Sigi a bicycle," she says, "and he will go to the country and also climb the *Berge*."

"Not an automobile?" I inquire, trying to put her on.

"Nein, nein," she says. "Walking is better. Legs are not only to sit on."

In early July, three weeks before our departure from Germany, the English Seminar of the university went on an all-day outing to see a baroque church, climb a hill, and have dinner at a country inn. There were some thirty-five of us: two of the Seminar's professors, a number of their assistants, a few faculty wives, students, and members of the clerical staff. We went in individual cars to our destination.

The church itself is located on a lovely green rolling hill. Its facade is undeniably interesting but, to my *Kultur*-uninitiated

eyes, the inside is a colossal disappointment, a baroque bore.
Who can pray in such a gingerbready place, amid sprightly an-
gels and cherubim and flamboyant alabaster balconies? A
learned discourse on the historic significance of the place in the
development of church architecture left me cold. Finally, I
slipped out of an exit and had coffee and a torte in an adjoining
café. Yes, call me vulgar, but if I must choose between such baroque and *essen,* give me *essen* any time.

Later we hiked up a steep road to the top of a high hill. From
up there we had a good view of villages, farmland, churches,
monasteries. Along the way, I spoke with some of the students.
They were openly bitter about the general state of German
higher education. It wasn't merely the University of Erlangen
they found fault with but rather the university system as a
whole. They criticized the overcrowded student enrollments, the
shortage of professors, the unrealistic nature of the curric-
ula, certain inequities in the final examinations, the excessive
number of years in residence required for a teaching certificate,
the lack of adequate libraries. Some complained about the au-
thoritarian conduct of German professors and their exploitation
of easily intimidated assistants. All of them expressed a keen
desire to study in the United States. They had heard that American professors were affable and democratic, and it was their
fantasy that American students were not made to feel they were
an unimportant part of a mass-production educational factory.

Our appetites whetted on country *Luft,* we hiked back down
to an inn. There we sat around an immensely long table, professors beside students, secretaries beside teaching assistants. If au-
thoritarian practices exist in the German university system, it
was not in evidence on that occasion. All appeared convivial,
lighthearted. The food and wine were fine. *Gemütlichkeit*
prevailed.

I was ill at ease. A good amount of the general conversation,
which was largely conducted in English, dwelt on church art
and music, as though on such occasions it were good form for
members of an academic community to demonstrate their intel-

lectual interests in *Kultur*. I had the distinct feeling that both
the faculty and the students spoke with the kind of brittle preci-
sion that they gave to their table manners; as though there was
a one-to-one relationship between the way you carved up a
piece of cutlet and the nature of your sensibilities; as though
only a person who could gracefully balance his fork with ease
was qualified to speak with authority on Schiller, Hölderlin,
Goethe, Rilke, Bach, and Mozart.

Why such an ultraintellectualized, highly abstract emphasis
on *Kultur?* Did, for example, publicly stating one's allegiance to
baroque music automatically place one on the side of the guard-
ians of Culture and Tradition? But then Hitler and many of his
fellow criminals also stood foursquare behind poetry, chamber
music, baroque castles and churches. And the readiness to
shiver on hearing Mozart did not prevent many a Third Reich
German from destroying innocent human beings. Yes, to cast
about high-level intellectual abstractions is all very nice and
useful, but were the conversationalists equally in touch with the
concrete, sentient human qualities—what Saul Bellow calls the
"exactly human"—in themselves? I had the impression—perhaps it was grossly inaccurate—that throughout this extended
conversation on Art and the Spirit, their heads were finely tuned
up, while their emotions stayed in deepfreeze.

But I press too much what may well have been superficial observations of the table talk. There was, as I said, no question
about the excellence of the food and especially the wine. After
downing a third glass of it, I stopped worrying about whether
my fork and knife were conducting themselves in good form.
Thus a day of *Kultur* and togetherness in the great Bavarian
outdoors.

I sat a few yards from where Hitler once stood in Zeppelin
Wiese. On the following day we would be leaving Nuremberg,
and I wanted a last glimpse of this vestige of Third Reich
"history." For the half hour of my stay there, no one entered the
deteriorating stands of the stadium. And no one was in the

weedy field below, where once the earth had trembled under the heels of 100,000 Nazi marchers.

Sitting there, I was in a frame of mind to judge not only Hitler and his followers but myself. "Why didn't you care?" I asked myself. For wasn't I among the silent ones in the early '40's while millions of innocent people were being destroyed? Why silent? Partly because I didn't know what was happening in Europe. But, more pointedly, because I hadn't identified with European Jewry. Granted, as an Army Air Corps technician during World War II, I did a job in the fight against Hitler. But apart from such a standardized commitment, I hadn't had any knowledgeable sense of European Jews. Stetl? Hasid? *Kiddush ha-shem?* Kishinev? Well, several times I happened to come upon these exotic-looking words in print or heard elderly Jews refer to them. But in those days such references bored me— boredom comes easily to the uninformed. The point is that I really didn't know *what* European Jewry was. Such understanding would have involved being at least minimally knowledgeable about Jewish history. Nor can such ignorance be excused on the grounds that during the years of the Final Solution I was in my early twenties. Surely that was old enough for my pillow to have burned because the Temple was burning; old enough to have known something about the question of Jewish identity, and to have understood the familiar saying that all Jews are responsible for one another.

Also—this is incredible—I can't remember having been distressed on first reading of the Warsaw ghetto uprising. Was the story buried in an obscure place of the newspaper? Can I now alibi that no one pointed out to me the tragic implications of this event? That if, say, a Jew had been present in my air base to speak about the heroism of the ghetto fighters, I might not have reacted with zero feelings to the news reports on the Uprising?

Well, even granting this possibility, where were my feelings when the first stories on the liberation of the death camps were reported in the newspapers and over the radio? I do not remember having felt sorrow or anger or even incredulity. Oh, at best perhaps an abstracted reaction of concern. But certainly no immediate scorching sense of pain that might discomfort me for at least a few hours. A glance at the news reports and then my mind journeyed to matters that were much closer at hand: a steak dinner at the noncom's club, a movie at the PX, a date with some readily available girl in the nearby town. Why not? Because what special ties did I have to the grotesque skeletons that the Allied armies had "liberated"? Besides, I cerebralized, others had also suffered, had they not? The people of Lidice, the Russians. . . . Yes, I was warmly clad and well fed while my fellow Jews in Europe were starving and dying in mass graves and gas chambers. So can I now self-righteously point a finger of accusation at those Germans who felt so little or nothing when the facts of the camps were forcibly brought to their attention during the months following the end of the war?

Recalling the nature of this moral blackout during the '40s, I began to perceive a little more clearly why I had come to Germany. Perhaps I had had the need to *enter* the Holocaust, in the sense intended by Elie Wiesel's statement: "Any German or Jew who was born before, during or after the Holocaust must enter it again in order to take it upon himself." ("Jewish Values in the Post-Holocaust Future," *Judaism,* Summer, 1967, p. 285.) Until I entered Germany, I had not truly felt on my pulses the tragedy of the Holocaust; oftener than not Dachau had seemed to me, as it still does for many young Germans, ancient history. It was as though we, these young Germans and I, had been afflicted by an amnesia concerning the Hitler years. Yet until we "entered" that "lost" time and "took it upon ourselves," we would not be able to know what our unique obligations are to each other as Germans and Jews. We need to determine where Dachau is in us now.

Our VW stood in the street before the Baier house, the oversize top rack bulging with suitcases. We were ready to begin the long journey to Naples and from there by ferry boat to Israel. I

had a year's sabbatical leave from my college to do research on
Holocaust literature at the Yad Vashem Archives in Jerusalem.

Behind us were memories of a fine weekend on the ski slopes
of Garmisch, three days in Berchtesgaden, a walk around the
ramparts of the old wall in Rothenburg, delightful visits to the
zoo, the Kaiserburg, Dutzendteich, and museums and parks in
Nuremberg. Good memories, too, of the Chinese tea garden in
the Englischer Garten of Munich, the Margrave's Place at Ans-
bach, the fortress and residence of Würzburg, the castle in Göss-
weinstein, Dinkelsbühl and swans floating on the waters of a
moat. A cycle of almost eleven months since that first morning
we had arrived in Nuremberg from Paris, and now we were on
our way out.

A little girl, blond and pony-tailed, about Dina's age, quietly
stood on the sidewalk watching us. Marie lived across the street.
It was only in the last month of our stay that this girl's mother
had encouraged her shy daughter to play with Dina. Until then,
the two girls had never spoken five consecutive words to each
other in a commonly understood language, and yet now Dina
was referring to the other as "my friend." "My friend Marie is
sad because I'm leaving."

Dina could have said the same thing of Frau Baier, who was
taking our going very hard. In the week before our departure,
she wept openly and often. Dina, she said, had become like a
daughter to her, and Tam like a younger sister. And now she
stood on the sidewalk, beside Marie, looking at us with a funereal expression. Herr Baier and Sigi had already said good-by
to us and were sitting before one of the upstairs windows on the
second floor.

The sky looked gray, spent, as it had on the day of our arrival in Nuremberg.

When the VW began rolling, I looked in the rearview mirror.
Frau Baier and Marie, side by side, like sculptured figures symbolizing the younger and older generations, seemed very distant
and small against the gray gabled houses and the sullen sky.
Our kids were waving through the back window. There were

tears in Tam's eyes. We turned a corner and the two figures at
the end of the street disappeared.

It was about a three-hour drive to Munich. As we drove
along the autobahn, I had some relatively quiet moments in
which to muse on the future possibilities for a democratic Germany. A disturbing story that I had heard only the week before
came back to me. It seems that a Jewish girl in Munich had appeared for a job interview, and the prospective employer was
reluctant to hire her, finally admitting that he feared some of his
customers might object to dealing with a Jew. The girl was
shocked, and she threatened to sue the man. Whereupon the
German employer went into a rage and said that he had been
misunderstood, that some of his best friends were Jewish, etc.,
etc. But other Germans didn't feel that way, *other* Germans
were intolerant. Later the girl said that the incident made her
feel what it must be like to be a Negro in certain places of the
United States.

There were other discouraging reports. A leading German
politician had publicly declared that "not a single Jew had been
gassed on German soil." He repeated the story that the gas
chambers had been erected by the Americans after the war "to
blacken Germany in the eyes of the world." This same man,
asked for his opinion of Hitler, replied: "It is too early to give a
historical judgment. A great deal of dirt was thrown at Napo-
leon in the first years after his death." And other voices inside
Germany have asserted that the "hour of forgiveness had come,
even for those with blood on their fingers." These alarming reports made me wonder what, for one, German college students
and their professors would do if there should be a resurgence of
a neo-Nazi movement in the country. Would they publicly protest or remain silent? Would they opt to walk through the
streets of ultraconservative communities carrying placards that
condemned the emergence of new Hitlers? Perhaps they would
remain silent.

On the other hand, there were numerous encouraging signs.

For one, a public meeting in Frankfurt where some young Germans spoke enthusiastically about their summer's journey to Israel and played Hasidic songs. Suddenly, in the midst of this account, a man stood up and triggered a noisome monologue on how inhuman and rotten the Jews have been to the Arabs, letting them starve in the refugee camps, letting them rot in temporary housing barracks, and denying them restitution. Jumping up, a man with an obvious Jewish name execrated Nasser. Another man, identifying himself as a Jew, turned to the German who had harangued against Israelis and said something to the effect that before he would let him decide who was inhuman, he would spit in his face. It took several minutes before the students managed to restore order.

It was encouraging to hear that these German Jews were not timid about speaking out in public places. Perhaps such an incident was an indicator that the self-conscious hothouse love for Jews in Germany was coming to an end—and it must come to an end if the proper conditions for an authentic dialogue between Germans and Jews are to emerge.

I anticipated the skeptical tone in which our friends back home would inquire, "Do you really think the Germans have changed, or that they even can change?" In response, I could refer them to the story of Dr. Janusz Korczak, the late Polish-Jewish educator and director of the Jewish orphanage in Warsaw. On August 5, 1942, he and some two hundred children of the orphanage were ordered by the SS to be taken away for "resettlement." So he placed himself at the head of the children, and they marched through the streets of Warsaw toward the transport singing, "We are all brothers"—followed by a German guard. It is known that the Judenrat offered him an opportunity to avoid deportation, but he rejected their offer and entered the train cars with his children. They were never seen again. And twenty-some years later, on Martyrs and Heroes Remembrance Day in Jerusalem, Israeli children come home from school wearing replicas of the disgraceful badges that Jews were forced to wear in Nazi-occupied countries. Underneath the stars appear the words of Korczak—and perhaps they would offer a reply to our friends' question—"There is no end to the desire for goodness. Out of this desire will come the fruit." And then I would tell them about some of the young Germans whom we had met. . . .

As we drove south, past Munich, into Austria and through the Alps, Tam and I remembered that years before, Jews from the European D.P. camps had come this way en route to a new life in Israel. With this difference: we were going there in safety and comfort. We had a car, no shortage of traveler's checks and more than one change of clothes for each of us, as compared with the hard road taken by the displaced survivors. Carrying their clothes on their backs, they journeyed cross-country by night and through forests to avoid detection by frontier guards. On occasion, in the dead of winter, they were forced to proceed on foot. Sometimes children and the elderly had to be carried through the snow of the Alps. Stronger hands than theirs would lift them up icy slopes. Many did not live to reach the ships waiting in Italian waters to bring them to Israel.

We did not feel at ease until we were beyond Germany and Austria. All through the weeks before our departure, Tam and I had been unable to shut out a persistent irrational fear that we would not be allowed to leave Germany without paying some sort of price. One of us would fall critically ill . . . there would be a horrible accident, either in Nuremberg or along the road. . . . Millions of Jews killed by Germans, so why should we be permitted to leave the country unscathed? I kept a firm grip on the wheel and tensely watched the oncoming drivers. It was only when our car crossed over the Austrian border that we began to relax. A guard cleared us to enter Italy.

The sun was shining on the road ahead. Italy and a sea voyage to Israel were before us. We all touched hands for good luck. None of us looked back. Dina asked how far it was to Beersheba and the camels.

EPILOGUE

IN ISRAEL, shortly after we arrived there from Germany, an Israeli poet said to Tam and me: "Let Germans come here, if they need to. But I myself would not go there. And I certainly do not think we Israelis ought to allow the works of our writers to appear on their radio and TV programs. Literature is the soul of a nation. After what they did to our people, it would not be proper for us to bring our soul to them. Perhaps in ten, fifteen years. But not now. And there is another reason. If we go there, they will think that Israelis are solicitous, self-demeaning. Let them not think here comes the Jew again, ready to shake hands. Kick him in the face and he still seeks your goodwill. Let them see that we are not ready to grasp their hands, no matter what the bribe." A short while before our conversation, my host had said No to a radio station in Hamburg that had asked him to send some of his poems for reading over the air.

Similarly, veteran *kibbutzniks,* men and women with reputation for tolerance and fairness, told us that they did not want German repentants at their settlements. "Why do they come here?" a young woman angrily asked us. "We don't want them. If they want to do some good, let them stay home and work so that another Hitler will never arise in their country." A number of her relatives had been killed in Europe during the Holocaust. And Tam and I saw Israeli students bristle and turn away at the suggestion that they ought to demonstrate trust and goodwill to German repentants in Israel. One such student, having read that the majority of Germans did not want to extend the Statute of Limitations, said to us, "Their coming here to work and repent reminds me of the man who goes to church to pray while his saloon and house of prostitution are operating at full blast."

That Israelis should mistrust even the younger generation of Germany was understandable; yet I could not always agree that their suspicions were justified. I would speak of the worthy young people whom we had met in Germany and of their honest sense of moral obligation to the Jewish people. And, as our stay in Israel lengthened, we were able to offer testimony on the achievements of some young Germans who were working on kibbutzim and on building projects in the cities. Specifically, Tam and I were impressed by the work of Aktion Sühnezeichen ("Service of Reconciliation"), a German organization of volunteers working in Israel and also in European countries that had suffered from the Nazi occupation.

We first came to know of this remarkable organization during a visit to Ahavah, an institution in Kiryat Bialik providing specialized care for children. It was there that we met the leader of the group, a young man who to our eyes—at the time we had been in Israel for only a week—looked like a native. We asked the way to the director's office. He had some difficulty in speaking English; after discovering that we knew a little German, he gave us directions in that tongue.

A few months before, Herzel and nineteen other members of Aktion Sühnezeichen had arrived in Israel. At the time of our visit, he and fifteen others were working in Kibbutz Hassolelim in the lower Galilee; that day he had come from Hassolelim to visit with the four young women who were on the staff at Ahavah. In Germany he had been a social worker in a church-sponsored community welfare program.

The presence of the man staggered us. A powerful radiance burned in his eyes. His face recalled the deeply inward and intense face in photographs of the Jewish visionary, Theodor

Herzl, to whom his name bears startlingly close resemblance.

Tam and I mentioned that we had just come from Germany and that we were in Israel because my college had granted me a sabbatical leave to do research on Holocaust literature. Herzel spoke quietly, calmly; he related no more than a few facts about the nature and objectives of Aktion Sühnezeichen. We said that we wanted to see him again and to meet the others in his group; and so he invited us to come for a day's visit to Hassolelim.

In its isolated location, a few miles to the northwest of Nazareth, this community is not in a Garden of Eden setting. The stony land surrounding the kibbutz appears—at least it did so on the gray, overcast day of our visit—sternly austere, almost surly, as though obdurately resisting the efforts men were making to transform it into greenness. The kibbutz was comparatively young in years, its membership fairly small.

Shortly after our arrival, we found Herzel in the kitchen of the dining hall, washing trays, silverware, plates; his sleeves were rolled up and sweat was streaming down his face. He explained that as he had to work in the kitchen for another hour, two English-speaking members of the group would show us around the kibbutz. Presently two young men led us off on a tour.

One of our guides gave us a brief account of the history of Aktion Sühnezeichen. The organization came into being on April 30, 1952, during the annual meeting of the Evangelical Synod in Berlin. At the outset, Judge Lothar Kreyssig, a leading official of the Evangelical Church in Germany, delivered an urgent summons to action. He argued that perhaps Germany could reduce some of the world's animosity against them for having started World War II by pleading for forgiveness and putting the plea into practice. He hoped that those countries which had suffered the most from the war would allow Germans to work there with their hands. Following Judge Kreyssig's summons, the membership of the organization, at first largely drawn from the student community in Berlin and supported by church institutions and community agencies, began to prepare for active work abroad. Before leaving Germany, volunteers received an orientation course on the history of the country to which they had been assigned and on the history of Germany from 1933 to 1945. From March 31 to June 26, 1959, the first group worked in Norway and Holland, planting trees. Thereafter, other groups built an international youth center in Coventry, England, a youth center in Holland, a Jewish community center in France. In 1963 another group built two classroom buildings for blind children in Jerusalem. In early 1965 a group worked at Kibbutz Magall. Meanwhile, hundreds of others in Germany had applied for a year's assignment to Israel. However, the guide was quick to add that as yet the organization had no mass appeal. "We are only a few," he emphasized. "Also, we realize that to build a children's home or work on a kibbutz doesn't begin to atone for what the Jewish people suffered. What we are doing here is very little. Still, it is a beginning, a small step, and others will come after us."

After our partial tour of the kibbutz, while we were resting under some trees in a field, the Aktion Sühnezeichen members, among them five young women, began appearing. They were attractive-looking, their faces without a sign of the boredom and self-indulgence one observes among American and European youth. In Germany they had been students, mechanics, carpenters, white-collar workers. Herzel was the last to arrive.

In the lengthy conversation that followed we were, I believe, candid with one another. Certainly they spoke up on what they didn't like about Israelis. A young man said: "Why *must* clerks in public offices snap at you, even before you have had a chance to finish asking the simplest of questions? Why must so many people be impolite? Please don't misunderstand. We have much admiration for the youth of Israel. But it's true that they are full of bad manners. Still, maybe it's better that way—better than the way we were raised: you know, where the child is supposed to be seen, but not heard, and the rod is not spared. Because see how stiffly polite Germans are—sometimes hypocritically so. That's one thing we really appreciate about Israeli youth. When they have something on their mind, they tell it to you—to your face. There's no sham in them."

At the outset I asked the group, "What is it you have learned thus far from your stay here?" A young man replied: "I am impressed by the way Israelis work hard, the love they have for their country, and their readiness to fight for it. In Germany we sometimes heard, from the older people, that Jews did not want to work with their hands. I would like to show these people how on our kibbutz Israelis lift tons of rocks out of the ground, sometimes with their bare hands. And I would like them to see how closely identified Israelis are with the problems of the country. They really care. If there is a drought, not only the farmer feels it. The city man worries for the farmer. When did I, living in Düsseldorf, ever get excited when the rains came, because it was good for the country? And I have heard a bus driver speaking about *his* army, as though it were someone in his own family."

Toward the midpoint in the conversation, Tam and I voiced our largest grievance against several young people we had met at a dinner party in a Nuremberg home, namely, their attitude toward the continuing presence of German scientists in Egypt who were helping Egyptians to build long-range missiles that could be directed against Israeli cities. "How do you feel about the possibility that for the second time in this century Germans could be responsible for the destruction of Jews?" we had asked them. And one young man, speaking for the others, had replied: "According to the law, every citizen has the right to work where he wants. So there is nothing we can do about it. The government decides," he had said casually. "Besides, you Americans don't tell your people where they can and cannot work, do you? So why should it be any different here?"

Their response had irritated us. After the destruction of millions of people by Germans, how could they reply with the jurisprudential head and not the outraged heart! They were oblivious to the moral principle involved. Theirs was the reply of those who perennially choose not to choose and therefore cannot be held blameless for the results of their passivity, inaction.

Fortunately, it was not necessary for us to belabor the point for the benefit of the group at Hassolelim; they informed us that Aktion Sühnezeichen has consistently taken a strong stand against the presence of such Germans in Egypt.

Although most of the group had to return to work, four young men were available to conduct us through the rest of the kibbutz—"*our* kibbutz," they kept referring to it. They particularly enjoyed showing us the cow barns and the bin where sheep are sheared. In explaining the process of shearing to us, they were obviously amused and pleased to hear themselves talking like genuine farmers. Heretofore, as city dwellers, none of them had ever before cleaned out sheep bins or milked cows. In the beginning, the sun, the diet, and the six-day work week had been hard on them, and two or three of their group had seriously considered returning to Germany. But all of them had stayed on, become good workers, and won the respect of veteran *kibbutzniks,* among them a former German Jew, a concentration camp survivor.

Apart from their labor, there were other ways in which they were giving an account of themselves as members of Aktion Sühnezeichen. They related some of their encounters away from Hassolelim. Traveling around the country on their free days, they generally chose to hitchhike rather than to ride buses. On hearing who they were, some drivers immediately became close-mouthed and the remainder of the ride would be passed in an awkward silence. But they realized that such rebuffs were a small price to pay for being Germans in a country full of people who had been marked by the Holocaust. Here one of the young men said: "If a German comes to visit Israel and is treated badly by some of the people, he has no right to complain. That is a small price he must pay for being a German—small, indeed, compared to the fate the Jewish people suffered. If he can't put up with the feeling of not being liked—and we Germans find it necessary to be liked by everybody—let him return to Germany."

Then two of our guides told us of the former Auschwitz prisoner who had stopped his car to give them a lift. On hearing who they were, the first Germans he had spoken to in many years, he was incredulous. "But when we explained why we were in Israel, he was unable to let us go and insisted on driving back to our kibbutz. We invited him to have dinner with us. Afterward we sat in the dining hall, talking late into the evening. He spoke about what had happened to him in Europe, the loss of his entire family. It was horrible, the sorrow of this man. It was the first time we had ever heard a Jew talk about the Holocaust. I don't think we have ever felt more ashamed of being Germans. There wasn't anything we could say. . . . We had only to listen. And there had been thousands like him in Germany. Such people we threw out and murdered! Before leaving, he shook each of our hands and said it was good that we were in Israel. But the look of suffering in his eyes when he took our hands! We shall never forget him."

"Do you think that there is something doomed in the German people?" one of the other young men asked with a troubled expression, not really addressing the question to Tam and me but rather to some place within himself. "Perhaps there is a sickness in us we will never be able to be rid of. Something that accounts for why we have turned from time to time to such inhuman acts against humanity. You talked about this before, the way those people from Nuremberg said that the German scientists in Egypt were not their responsibility. Why are we always so slow to *feel* the moral principle involved in the affairs of others?"

Later, as Tam and I were preparing to leave the kibbutz, Herzel bid us shalom, saying, "We thank you for the visit and for your readiness to witness our work toward reconciliation." He paused. "I don't know how it will be for us when we return to Germany—whether our friends and relatives will understand why we went to Israel. But I can tell you this: we promise to keep speaking out."

And they probably have. In any event, since then I have often thought of them. They were on my mind when I read about the tremendous outpouring of public concern and financial support for Israel from Germans, of every age and calling, during and after the Six Day War. Placards appeared in the streets: "Are Six Million Victims Not Enough?" Hundreds of young Germans volunteered to fight on the side of Israel. I recalled Herzel and his group on reading a newspaper account of how thousands of Germans marched through university towns in protest against the right-wing National Democratic Party, alleged by some political commentators to be a potential successor to the Nazi movement. By contrast with the older generation's exaggerated respect for authority and obedience, these protestors evidently do not feel that the first duty of citizens is to keep silent. Walking through the streets, they were saying with their bodies: no more Hitlers, no more killing of Jews.

Altogether, from going over voluminous written material on postwar Germany, I have the impression that the younger generation there, far from wanting to "forget," is honestly trying to come to grips with the National Socialist past. True, doubtless many, weary of still living under the shadow of Hitler, have repressed feelings of guilt and shame. Nevertheless, it is my understanding that the vast majority of German youth are willing to talk about the Holocaust, to bring the tragic facts on this history into the open. Hence they continue to raise the significant questions: What actually happened? How is it possible that Germans behaved so inhumanely? What can we do to help bring about a more democratic Germany? Such ongoing questioning I regard as a very good sign.

Promising, too, are the reports that Tam and I have received from some young Nurembergers on their trips to Israel. They visited the Chamber of Destruction on Mt. Zion in Jerusalem, a public memorial to the Holocaust dead. There they stood silently looking down at a marble slab inscribed with the names of concentration camps like Auschwitz and Dachau, and covering the ashes of Jews from twenty-two European communities. On the stone walls of this room are plaques listing the names of towns and cities in Europe where Jews no longer live.

In a corner, within a glass case, are the remains of a flame-scarred Torah. The point was not lost on these visitors that such Torahs were housed in German synagogues.

They made special mention of a visit to the Beit Katznelson Museum at Lohamei Hagetaot, the Fighters of the Ghettos Kibbutz in the Western Galilee, a settlement founded in 1949 by survivors (among them the great hero of the Warsaw ghetto uprising, Antek) of Polish and Lithuanian communities. This museum contains records and relics of the death camps and European ghettos.

However, what moved the visitors was not the collection of illustrated horrors inside the museum but rather what they saw immediately on leaving it: orange groves and banana fields stretching out serenely from the kibbutz to the distant hills of Galilee. Not too many years before this land had been neglected, barren; hard work had made it bloom. Looking at the green landscape before them, these young Germans were able to realize that the settlers of this kibbutz have made a long journey from the places of yellow badges and barbed wire in Europe.

When such travelers return to Germany, they do so with an awakened understanding, as a young woman wrote to us in summing up her year's stay in Israel.

> Now, coming from Israel, we have more open eyes. The worst thing with the German people is that they look on this problem of German-Jewish reconciliation in too passive a way and don't want to bear the responsibility. And even if we young people don't want to, the fact is we belong to this people and are connected insolubly with its history, with what happened. So long as we have to live together with the murderers that took part in the atrocities, we have to feel responsible for our own folk and to care for a better and cleaner future.
>
> These are big words for so small a person like me but it is what I am thinking. Now we have to be cautious against becoming what they call pro-Semites. And this

is what I fear—that I am going to be a pro-Semite, because I like so much the Israelean people and I found a great sympathy with the Jewish religion. But I hope that this will be no danger for our work here. This is what I wanted to tell you. Shalom.

The crimes committed by Germans during the Hitler years cannot be made "good." The dead cannot be brought to life again. Even so, it seems to me that some critics of today's Germany are themselves of too little faith—Korczak's kind of faith—to perceive the possibilities for meaningful reconciliation between Germans and Jews. Here it is instructive to read what Rabbi Joseph Asher has stated in an article, "Isn't It Time We Forgave the Germans?" (*Look,* April 20, 1965): "In looking at Germany, I can see that there can be no genuine and lasting rehabilitation without rehabilitation on a person-to-person level. The horror of it all is too great to grasp; it eludes us. The small inhumanities, however, are within our power to heal. . . . As wickedness springs from small and individual acts, thus does compassion begin in a single man's heart." In a similar vein, the world-renowned scholar Professor Gershom Scholem has written in a much-discussed essay, "Jews and Germans" (*Commentary,* November, 1966):

> Today there are many Jews who regard the German people as a "hopeless case," or at best as a people with whom, after what has happened, they want nothing to do, for good or ill. I do not count myself among them, for I do not believe that there ought to be such a thing as a permanent state of war among peoples. I also deem it right—what is more, I deem it important—that Jews, precisely, *as* Jews, speak to Germans in full consciousness of what has happened and of what separates them. (P. 31.)

Granting the difficulties of such dialogue, Professor Scholem goes on to say:

> Fruitful relations between Jews and Germans, relations
> in which a past that is both meaningful and at the same
> time so horrible as to cripple communication may be
> preserved and worked through—such relations must be
> prepared with great care. But it is only through an effort
> to bring them about that we can guarantee that official
> contacts between the two peoples will not be poisoned
> by counterfeit formulas and demands. Already the worm
> of hypocrisy is gnawing at the delicate roots. Where love
> is no longer possible, a new understanding requires other
> ingredients: distance, respect, openness and openmind-
> edness, and above all, good-will on both sides. (P. 38.)

"I do not believe that there ought to be such a thing as a permanent state of war among peoples." To this I would add that it is imperative for open-minded men to challenge the prejudiced view that Germans "will *never* change." To look on the German people with such unbending distrust is perhaps to be marked by some of the poisoned hubris that the Nazis directed against those whom they labeled as *Untermenschen*. (Is there not a relationship between such dehumanizing phrases reportedly used by GI's who participated in the My Lai slaughter, such as "the only good dink is a dead dink," and the familiar epithets of American racists, or, for that matter, the inflammatory rhetoric, e.g., pig administrators, student bums, faculty troublemakers, used by extremists on either side of the faculty barricades?) Now I am hardly equating the two kinds of prejudice: one led to murder and the other, at worst, represents an unjustified closed-mindedness. Nor am I suggesting that Jews fall all over themselves in reaching out for friendship with Germans. What is wanted is a balanced position of realistic mediation, one that avoids the extremes of fixed prejudice and instant reconciliation. What is wanted, in the words of Professor Scholem, is that Jews and Germans, precisely *as* Jews and Germans, speak to one another "in full consciousness of what has happened and of what separates them."

I have referred to the hope expressed by a University of Göttingen student that "only individual Germans confronting individual Jews can help to heal the wounds of the past." I agree. One afternoon during our stay in Israel, I observed some Israeli children at the Institute for the Blind in Jerusalem reaching out their hands uncertainly toward several members of an Aktion Sühnezeichen group that was constructing some classroom buildings on the grounds. *"Mi ze?"* [Who is this?] the blind children asked. Over the sounds of Peter, Ulrich, Willy, Diedrich, I heard one of the volunteers call out, *"Hinneni"* [Here I am], the reply from Genesis, from the depths, to the immemorial Biblical question: "Where are you?" And then, these young Germans went to a yard, picked up tools, and began working on the foundation for a new building.

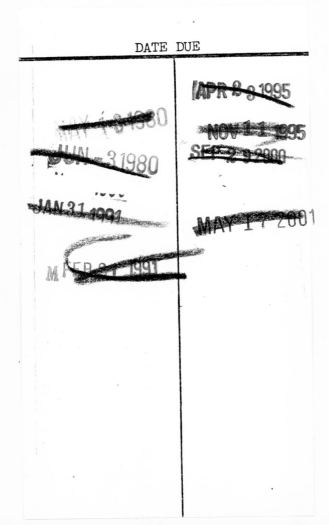